A Scots
Dictionary
of Nature

Amanda Thomson

A Scots
Dictionary
of Nature

Amanda Thomson

Saraband

Published by Saraband,
Suite 202, 98 Woodlands Road,
Glasgow, G3 6HB

and

Digital World Centre, 1 Lowry Plaza
The Quays, Salford, M50 3UB
www.saraband.net

ISBN: 9781912235186

10 9 8 7 6 5 4 3 2 1

Printed and bound in the EU on sustainably sourced paper.

*ILLUSTRATIONS: Branchers (title page); bogware (dedication page);
drystane dyke (contents page); skathie (page 223); dike-hopper (last
page); and otherwise as captioned next to the image.
All photographs are © Amanda Thomson, 2018.*

Amanda Thomson is a visual artist and writer who teaches at the Glasgow School of Art. She graduated with a first from Glasgow School of Art and has an MFA from the School of the Art Institute of Chicago. Her arts-based PhD, from UHI/ the University of Aberdeen, is about the forests of Abernethy and Morayshire. Her artwork is often about notions of home, movement and migration, landscapes and how places come to be made. She lives and works in Glasgow and in Strathspey. *A Scots Dictionary of Nature* is her first book.

for
mum
in memory of
gran and papa

Contents

About *A Scots Dictionary of Nature* .... *i*

Introduction *1*

1 Land *9*

2 Wood *93*

3 Weather *115*

4 Birds *141*

5 Water *167*

6 Walking *195*

Sources *225*

Acknowledgements *227*

About *A Scots Dictionary of Nature*

This book brings together traditional Scots words about nature in a way that has never been done before. Despite the title, it is not, in fact, a dictionary – at least not in the traditional sense. It is not intended to be a scholarly work of lexicography; instead, it is a collection of "found" words and archaic definitions compiled by an artist seeking to explore, curate, celebrate and preserve for posterity those words of the Scots language relating to the world around us.

There are three main sources – Jamieson's *A Dictionary of The Scottish Language* (1846), *Supplement to Jamieson's Scottish Dictionary* (1887) and *The Scots Dialect Dictionary* (1911) – and each of these source dictionaries had different approaches and ways of presenting their words and definitions. Every effort has been made to keep to the original wording and style of definitions, but if each entry were also to be presented in the original manner, it would soon get very messy indeed! And so, for the sake of clarity, some consistency of presentation has been applied to each of the entries.

Nevertheless, the use of various sources has led, inevitably, to some idiosyncrasies within this book. For example, sometimes the

Latin name for plants and birds is given, at other times it is not. Some entries feature examples of how the word is used in a sentence, many do not. There are variations in spelling, and the style of any given definition can vary greatly from that of another. In short, there are contradictions, inconsistencies and repetitions. And they are not only to be expected (given the differing primary sources), they are to be positively welcomed. For they are indicative of the depth, richness and variety of the Scots language and its unique relationship to nature and the Scottish landscapes of the Lowlands, Highlands and Islands. *A Scots Dictionary of Nature* is, first and foremost, a celebration of that language and its history.

Introduction

This *Scots Dictionary of Nature* has been a long time in the making. As an artist, much of my work is about the Scottish Highlands, and in 2010, when I made an artist's book called *A Dictionary of Wood* (which would be a first version of what you are reading now), I was doing research about the remnant Scots pinewood forests of Abernethy, and about Culbin, a Forestry Commission forest in Morayshire. Earlier that year, in a second-hand bookshop in Edinburgh, I had found an old Jamieson's A *Dictionary Of The Scottish Language*, abridged by John Johnstone and published in 1846. The original price of £11 was embossed in gold on the spine, and I bought it for £20. In opening random pages, I'd come across words such as *timmer breeks* (timber trousers), meaning a coffin, and *dedechack: the sound made by a woodworm in houses, so called from its clicking noise, and because vulgarly supposed to be a premonition of death.*

I loved these words and more: they had a resonance and a particular feeling to them that was sometimes poignant and affecting, and sometimes conveyed a prosaic descriptiveness that nonetheless spoke of close connections and an attentiveness to the nuances of the landscape, what it contains, how we move through it, and even specific times of day or year. *Break-back: the harvest moon, so called by the harvest labourers because of the additional work it entails.* There were also words like *huam: the moan of an owl in the warm days of summer*, evocative of that feeling of the haziness of a long, hot summer's day as it spills into evening. This old dictionary made me begin to wonder about lost connections to land and place and perhaps even ways of seeing and being in the world, and I began wondering what else I might find.

Eard-fast means *a stone or boulder fixed firmly in the earth*, or simply, *deep rooted in the earth*, and it's a word that seems to get to the heart of this book. It resonates with ideas of place and belonging, makes me think of deep connections to places and particular landscapes and makes me consider how language can assist or be at the root of such connections.

Between 2009 and 2013 I was doing a doctorate and an element of my research related to the gradual changes that happen over time in the forests of Morayshire and Abernethy and how, when one is familiar with a place, one sees many more layers and begins to recognise the subtlest of these changes. I was also interested in how we make sense of and articulate our relationships to the land, both visually and verbally. As I walked with foresters and ecologists, I came across words like *gralloch*, used by a deerstalker to describe the innards of a dead deer (and the verb *to gralloch*, which so viscerally describes the task of removing them). Such words were unfamiliar to me, and yet foresters and ecologists used them with ease and specificity to describe their everyday activities. As I listened and heard these new (to me) words, they informed additional ways of seeing and gave me different understandings of the places where I was walking and of the activities they were carrying out. And there were other phrases too, some quirky, others pithy. An older forester told me about a man who started working for the Forestry Commission but was not very good at his job: he was not "wid material", the forester said.

I decided to systematically go through the Jamieson dictionary looking for words related to wood, and did the same when I subsequently found a *Supplement to Jamieson's Scottish Dictionary*, edited by David Donaldson and published in 1887, and then a copy of *The Scots Dialect Dictionary*, edited by Alexander Warrack and published in 1911. I started making my way through each of these dictionaries, noting words – most of them completely unfamiliar – first in relation to wood, then over the years birds, weather, water, and of course, the land itself. The focus on words relating to walking came at a later date, as I began to think about how we discover places by moving through them; and how places themselves (and what we're doing in them) dictate how we move.

At the same time, there's also more of a personal connection. H.M. Steven and A. Carlisle, in *The Native Pinewoods of Scotland*, wrote "to stand in them is to feel the past", and in looking through these old Scots dictionaries there's a resonance with a different time as well as different connections to place, land, weather and, perhaps, a link to previous generations, both in the broadest sense, and in a more intimate and immediate sense. These are words we may remember our grandparents, or our great aunts and uncles, using. My maternal grandmother came from a place that my family calls The Haggs, but on maps it's just Haggs. It's a village just to the north of the Castlecary viaduct between Glasgow and Edinburgh, and to the east of the M80 motorway between Glasgow and Stirling. Fourteen family members lived in two small houses in a row of about five. The boys lived in one house, and my gran and her sisters lived with their parents in the other. The row is long demolished and must have sat somewhere above where the M80 now runs. They moved to a council house in Castleview Terrace in the 1940s, and my (great) Aunt Mary and two of her brothers lived there until they died, all of them well into their eighties. Accent and language always seemed to spill from west to east as we went from the town nearer Glasgow, where I was raised, to The Haggs, which had a more easterly lilt and used different words and intonations. I wish I remembered more, or had recorded them. I learn from looking at these old Scots dictionaries that *hagg* can mean *wild, broken ground* or *a piece of soft bog in a moor* or *a hole in a moss from which peats have been cut* or *a water-hollow, wet in winter and dry in summer* or *an islet of grass in the midst of a bog.* Then there's the *hag-wood: a copse wood fitted for having a regular cutting of trees.* I wonder which of these definitions, if any, best described the land where the village was originally built.

Words pull us together across borders and times. I have lovely conversations with a friend from Yorkshire, where we compare Scots and Yorkshire words. I always remember him telling me a story about his elderly father who had fallen down in his garden and couldn't get up. "Help!" he shouted, when he heard the postman at the door, "I'm rigwelted." The postman, also a Yorkshireman, heard his cry and knew to go and help him up, as *rigwelted* describes *a sheep stranded on its back*. I couldn't think of an equivalent word in Scots, and joked that perhaps our sheep just didn't fall down, but when I looked through these old dictionaries, there it was… *Awalt sheep: a sheep that has fallen on its back and cannot recover itself.*

I'm not a lexicographer, a linguist, or a historian of the Scottish language, but as an artist I am interested in words and language and how we might describe our world. In mining these dictionaries, I've found words that are rarely heard, no longer in use or perhaps largely forgotten. These "found" words evidence a confluence of local and social histories, allude to changing ways of life and shifting connections, and point to fascinating relationships with nature and the land. Some show how land and nature permeate other aspects of our lives. The word *flocht* relates to birds and means *on the wing*, but then there's *to flochter*, which means *to give free scope to joyful feelings*. Others give us immediate access to a language and a way of being in the world, being on and in the land, which may or may not be the same as now. While we see the same weather phenomena today, more or less, as when the Jamieson dictionary was published – over a century and a half ago – the impact and significance of particular kinds of weather is probably, for most of us, not the same. Naming denotes importance and significance, and the ability to notice *angry teth*[1], to recognise *Banff-baillies*[2], or to observe that the day is *lunkie*[3],

---

[1]   the fragment of a rainbow appearing on the horizon, and when seen on the north or east indicating bad weather

[2]   white, snowy-looking clouds on the horizon, betokening foul weather

[3]   denoting the oppressive state of the atmosphere before rain or thunder

has very different implications for car drivers or city-dwellers than for someone out in a small fishing boat or for a farmer assessing whether the barley should be harvested.

A collection such as this will always be partial. Jamieson's original work listed words from Older Scots (gleaned from earlier sources) as well as (his) contemporary Scots. Language, like our world, is responsive and in constant movement. There's a subjectivity, too, and some words placed in one section might equally sit in another, or several, and this speaks to the interrelatedness of our world. Some words can mean different things, sometimes dependent on locality. The word *flichter*, for example, means *a flake of snow* but it can also mean *a great number of small objects flying in the air, as a flichter of birds, a flichter of motes, etc.* Then the verb can also mean *to run with outspread arms, as children, to those they are much attached.* I am sure there are some relevant words in these dictionaries that I've missed, and I know also that there are words I've come across in other books that are not in these dictionaries and I've not included. "'A flinchin' Friday,' warned Miss Annie, who had a farmer's knowledge of the weather signs. 'There'll be a storm on the heels of this,'" Nan Shepherd writes in *The Weatherhouse*.

There's a beautiful poetry, but also a prosaic unsentimentality in some of the old Scots words that we have lost: *fir gowns, fir troosers* and *cauld-bark*, as well as *timmer breeks* are all words for coffin, and, together with words for the grave like *doon-lie, lang-hame* and *cauld-yird*, speak of a close connection to the earth, and the materials of the earth we use. There's a lovely drift, sometimes, between workaday descriptions and spillages into other, more preternatural realms. For example, the bird, the swallow: *In Teviotdale, this harmless bird is reckoned uncannie, as being supposed to have a "drap o' the de'il's bluid"; in other places, it is held a lucky bird and its nest is carefully protected; and the uncanniness is attributed, for the same potent reason, to the beautiful yorlin* (the yellowhammer). I wonder if there are still any *hellie-man's-rigs* about, *areas of land dedicated to the devil*, or where we might see *bar-ghaists*, these ghosts, *all in white, with large saucer eyes, appearing near gates or stiles.*

Some words evoke very specific phenomena, but also lovely connections. *Summer-couts* are *the gnats which dance in clusters on a summer evening,* or *the exhalations seen to ascend from the ground in a warm day.* A *startle-o'-stovie* also means *the undulating exhalations seen rising from the ground in very hot weather,* and then there's the verb, *to startle,* which means *to run wildly about, as cows do in hot weather,* and the word *stove,* which means a vapour, or a ground mist.

Occasionally, words and descriptions speak to time passing – for example the arrival of birds which herald a change in season, or even a very specific moment in a year: *a gowk's storm* is *a storm consisting of several days of tempestuous weather, believed by the peasantry periodically to take place about the beginning of April, at the time that the gowk, or cuckoo, visits the country,* then there's *a teuchit storm; the gale, in the reckoning of the vulgar, conjoined with the arrival of the green plover,* and *craw-Sunday; the first Sunday in March, on which crows were supposed to begin to build nests.*

In the wood section of this dictionary, I have of course included words for forests and trees and branches and growth, but, because of our close relationship to the materiality and functionality of wood I've also included objects made from wood, so there are *bossies, luggies, cogs, bickers, duddies, handies,* all wooden bowls, each with a different functions, and words like *tree-leggit,* meaning *having a wooden leg,* and *widdie-nek: gallows neck – one doomed to be hanged.*

So many words relate to ways of working that were different then to what they are now. We can see this in all the different words for ploughing and for the people who worked the land. Others speak of objects we no longer use. There's no need for *fir candles,* these splinters of wood with a high resin content that were cut from Scots pine trees and used to light homes. But there's more to this than words simply becoming redundant. The yellowhammer, a member of the bunting family, has been rapidly in decline over the past few decades, so much so that it is now a "red species", meaning that is endangered in the UK (although the numbers are better in Scotland), and it's thought that one of the reasons for this might be because changing agricultural practices have led to a decline in suitable habitats. Yet in these dictionaries there are eighteen different words for the yellowhammer (if we include slight spelling variations), suggesting that this is a bird which was once fairly common. In fact there is even a game mentioned in the Jamieson dictionary called *spangie-hewit*, described as being *a barbarous sport of boys to young Yellow-hammers*. And there's the yellowhammer as *the yorlin, thought to be uncannie, in some parts of the land.*

I am conscious that it is easy to look at these words and our affinity with the idea of this book as simple nostalgia or sentimentality, but it's more than that. Often we can see from these words just how hard life must have been and, anyway, nostalgia is a complicated thing. In *Nostalgia and its Discontents*, Svetlana Boym talks about how, while nostalgia might be longing for a place, it might also be a longing for a better time. She writes, "The word 'nostalgia' comes from two Greek roots, *nostos* meaning 'return home' and *algia* 'longing'." She goes on, "I would define it as a longing for a home that no longer exists or has never existed. Nostalgia is a sentiment of loss and displacement, but it is also a romance with one's own fantasy." Boym goes on to warn of the dangers of viewing the past through too narrow a prism, and she argues that we must take account of progress and newness, and I would say difference too. Boym also talks about the potential for a prospective nostalgia. She writes, "The fantasies of the past, determined by the needs of the present, have a direct impact on the realities of the future," and I wonder about the attentiveness to land and place evident in these old dictionaries. It seems apparent that we may have lost more than just words.

Like any other language, Scots not only changes with the passage of time, but encompasses regional variations, too.

Jamieson, where he was able to do so, listed the areas of Scotland where words were used, and he was very interested in tracing the earliest evidence of their use in that place. Some of his entries indicate very local usage – whether in Aberdeenshire, Shetland, Orkney, Ayrshire, Renfrewshire, etc. *The Scots Dialect Dictionary*, on the other hand, does not indicate place, and I've chosen not to put these specificities in this collection of words. I like the idea of their migration across places and time, where they belong to none of us and all of us. We might still use some of them, and some might remind us of our earlier selves or of people we miss. Some might make us think of how we used to live on the land and in nature, and of the lives of our ancestors, the *break-backs* and the *borrowing days*. Other words, however, might point to future ways of seeing the world, where we might take the time just to pause and look more, and see anew, or perhaps recognise familiar complications, joys and the elements of the world described differently. Perhaps to be around some of these words is *to cair: to return to a place where one has been before.*

Part one

Land

A

Aaron's-beard *n* the dwarf-shrub called St John's Wort: this plant was formerly believed by the superstitious in Sweden, as well as in Scotland, to be a charm against the dire effects of witchcraft and enchantment. By putting it into ropy milk suspected to be bewitched, and milking afresh upon it, they also fancied the milk would be cured.

acher *n* an ear of corn.

acherspyre *v* to shoot; to sprout; to germinate.

acher-dale *adj* divided into single acres or small portions.

acre-braid *n* the breadth of an acre.

adder-bead, -stane *n* the stone supposed to be formed by adders.

adder-bell, -cap *n* the dragon-fly.

adhantare *n* one who haunts a place.

adminacle *n* (perhaps) a pendicle of land.

ae-fur-land, ae-fur-brae *n* ground which, from its steepness, can be ploughed only in one direction, or with one furrow, the plough returning without entering the soil.

ae-pointit-gairss *n* sedge-grass, a species of carex; single-pointed grass.

aer, air, ayre *n* a sandbank or beach.

aff *adv, prep, adj* off; past; out of; from; from the direction of.

aff-ganging *v* (used of a tenant) leaving his farm.

afiel' *adv* abroad; in the fields; from home.

aft-crap *n, v* stubble-grass; after-math; to take two successive similar crops from the same field.

afterheid *n* grass in the stubble after harvest.

afterwald *n* that division of a farm called *outfield*.

agrest *adj* rustic; rural.

Agwet *n* the name anciently given to the hill on which the castle of Edinburgh stands.

ahame *adv* at home, within doors.

aicher *n* an ear of barley; a head of oats.

aikraw *n* pitted, warty lichen.

air-cock *n* a weather-cock.

aird *n* the earth; ground; soil.

airie *n* hill-pasture; an opening in the hills; a summer residence for herdsman; a sheiling.

airt *n, v* the quarter of the heavens; point of compass; the direction of the wind; a direction, way; (applied to the wind) to blow from a certain quarter.

airtan *n* direction; the placing towards a point of the compass.

aisle *v* to sun, to dry in the sun.

aislar-bank *n* a rocky bank, like ashlar work.

aiten *n* the juniper; the partridge.

aith, aiftland *n* that kind of land called *infield*, which was made to carry oats a second time after barley, and had received no dung.

aither *n* an adder.

aitliff crap *n* in the old husbandry, the crop after bear or barley.

aitnach *n* the juniper.

aits *n* oats; *wild aits*, bearded oat grass.

aitseed *n* oat-sowing; season of oat-sowing.

aiver *n* an old horse; a gelded he-goat.

allars *n* garden walks; alleys like garden walks.

allicompain *n* a medicinal plant greatly esteemed by country people in the West and South of Scotland, *Inula campana.*

Alshinder *n* Alexanders, a plant, *Smyrnium olusatrum.*

amerand *adj* green; verdant.

ana *n* a river-island; a holm.

anewis *n* budding flowers.

anying *n* (perhaps) the right of making hay on commons.

anyester *n* a two-year old sheep.

aplace *adv* in this place; here.

appen furth *phr* the free air, an open exposure.

arage, arrage, aryage, auarage, average *n* servitude due by tenants, in men and horses, to their landlords. This custom is not entirely abolished in some parts of Scotland, as in"arage and carriage", a phrase still commonly used in leases.

are, ere *v* to plough; to till.

arns *n* beards of corn.

arnut, arnot *n* tall oat-grass or pignut.

aron *n* the plant wakerobin, or cuckoo's-pint.

ask, awsk *n* an eft; a newt; a kind of lizard.

ask *n* the stake to which a cow is tied, by a rope or chain, in the byre.

asol, aisle, assol *n* sunning,

drying, mellowing or seasoning in the sun.

aten out o' ply *phr* animals that are very lean and in poor condition although they have an abundance of food are said to be "aten out o' ply", eaten out of plight or condition.

ather *n* an adder.

ather-bill, -cap *n* the dragon-fly. *See also* natter-cap.

athort *adv* through; across; abroad; far and wide.

atis *n* oats.

atour, at-owr *adv* across; over; at a distance away, as in "out-over".

attercap *n* a spider; an ill-natured person, one of a virulent or malignant disposition.

atween-lichts *phr* the distance between neighbours' houses.

averie *n* livestock, including horses, cattle, etc.

averin, averen, aivrin *n* cloudberry or knoutberry: eaten as a dessert in the north.

avil, awal, awald *n* the second crop after lea or grass; (applied to fields) lying the second year without being ploughed; lea of the second year that has not been sowed with artificial grasses.

awal-infield *n* the second crop after bear.

awal-land *n* ground under a second crop.

awald-crap *n* the second crop after *lea*.

awald-oats *n* the second crop of oats after grass.

awald, awalt sheep *adj* one that has fallen on its back and cannot recover itself: if not raised it sickens, swells and dies.

award-crap *n* a crop of corn after several others in succession; hence called *award* or *awkward* crops.

awat, awald *n* ground ploughed after the first crop from *lea*. The crop produced is called the *awat-crap*.

awastle *prep* to the westward of; figuratively, distant from.

a'where *adv* everywhere.

awned *adj* (applied to grain) having beards.

awns *n* the beards of corn; the beards of barley; a shoot or stalk.

awrige *n* the tips of the little ridges laid by the plough are called the *awrige* of the field: when the grain is sown the *awrige* is harrowed over to cover the seed.

ayont *adv* beyond.

B

baa *n* a rock in the sea seen at low water.

babbanqua *n* a quaking bog.

babie-pickle *n* the small grain (the *babie*) which lies in the bosom of a larger one at the top of a stalk of oats.

bachille *n* a pendicle or small piece of arable ground.

back-end o' hairst *phr* the latter part of the harvest.

back-owre *prep* behind; a considerable way back.

backe *n* the bat.

backit-dyke *n* a stone fence backed up with earth on the inner side.

bae *n, v* a bleat, the sound emitted in bleating; to bleat; to cry like a sheep.

bai *n* the cry of a calf.

baillie days *phr* days during which farmers were bound to labour for their lairds.

baittle *adj* denoting that sort of pasture where the grass is short, close and rich; also, fit for pasture.

balderry *n* female-handed orchis, a plant, *Orchis latifolia*.

baldie-worry *n* an artichoke.

balk and burral *n* a ridge raised very high by the plough and a barren space of nearly the same extent, alternately.

balk-bred, -braid *n* the breadth of a balk or ridge of unploughed land.

balkie *n* a narrow strip of land separating two farms.

balloch, belloch *n* a narrow mountain pass.

band *n* (used of a hill) the top or summit; the ridge of a small hill.

bandwin-rig *n* a ridge so broad that it can contain a band of reapers, called a *win*.

bane-fyre *n* a bonfire.

banks *n* precipitous rocks or crags near the sea-shore.

bar *n* barley.

bar awns *n* the beards of barley.

bar-ghaist *n* a ghost all in white, with large saucer eyes, appearing near gates or stiles.

barescrape *n* very poor land yielding little return for labour.

barley-bing *n* a heap of barley.

barnat *adj* native, the land of our *barnheid* or nativity, as in "our barnat land".

barr *n* a ridge of a hill; a large hill.

barried *adj* thrashed; stiff and sore as after a day's thrashing.

bassie *n* an old horse.

bassin *adj* of or belonging to rushes.

basties, bastish *adj* coarse; (applied to soil) hard, bound.

bat *n* a holm, a river island.

bathie *n* a booth or hovel; a summer sheiling.

battell *adj* rich for pasture.

battick *n* a piece of firm land between two rivulets, or two branches of the same river.

battock *n* a tuft of grass, a spot of gravel, or ground of any kind, surrounded by water.

baud, bawd *n* a quantity, or bed of whins growing closely together.

baudminnie, baldminny *n* a plant with the medicinal virtue of savin; the plant Gentian, believed to have properties that can kill the foetus in the womb, hence its name *bawd-money.*

bauk, bawk *n, v* a strip of land left unploughed, two or three feet in breadth; to leave small strips of land not turned up in ploughing.

baukie *n* the bat.

baulkie *n* a narrow strip of land separating two farms.

bawd *n* a hare.

bawsie *n* a horse or cow having a white strip or patch on the face.

bay *n* the sound caused by the notes of birds.

bayle-fire *n* a bonfire; any large fire.

be-east *adj, adv* eastwards.

beal *n* an opening between hills; a narrow pass.

bear, bere *n* barley, having four rows of grains.

bear-feys, -land *n* land appropriated to raising barley.

bear-lave, -leave *n* ground the first year after it has been cropped with bear.

bear-root, beer-root *n* the first crop after bear or barley.

bear-seed *n* barley; the time of sowing barley or of preparing the ground for it.

beast *n* a horse, cow, ox or sheep; a louse; the devil; any animal but man.

bee-bike *n* a wild bee's nest.

bee-stone *n* the stone on which a hive rests.

bee's wisp *n* a wild bee's nest on the surface of the ground.

beefer *n* an ox or cow fed for the butcher.

beel *n* a shelter; used of cattle, to collect them at night to a spot suitable for their spending the night in the open; a place they are so collected.

beetle-bee *n* a flying beetle; a humming beetle.

beetraw *n* beetroot.

beik *n, v* a nest of wild bees; a gathering; to bask in the sun.

beild *n, v* a shelter; on the side of the wall that is free from the blast, to shelter; to protect, as in "in the beild of the dyke".

beildless *adj* unsheltered.

beildy *adj* affording shelter; well-sheltered.

being, bing *n* the beach of the sea-shore.

Belfuff *n* an ideal hill supposed to be near *Heckie-* or *Hecklebirnie*, which is fabled to be three miles beyond hell.

bell *n* the blossom of a plant, as in "lint in the bell", flax in flower.

bell of the brae *n* the highest part of the slope of a hill.

bell-heather *n* cross-leaved heath.

belli-bucht *n* a hollow in a hill transverse to the slope.

belling *n, adj* the state of desiring the female; a term properly applied to harts.

bellis *n* (perhaps) the *belling-time* of beasts, mentioned above.

belt *n* often used to denote a strip of planting; a small narrow plantation.

ben *n* a mountain, used both in composition and by itself; a hill.

bennel *n* long, reedy grass, growing in stagnant waters.

benner gowan *n* the mountain daisy; the garden fever-few.

benorth *adj, adv* to the northward of.

bent *n* a coarse kind of grass, growing on hilly ground; common hair-grass; the coarse grass growing on the sea-shore; the open field, the plain.

bent-moss *n* a soil composed of firm moss covered with a thick herbage of *bent*.

bentiness *n* the state of being covered with *bent*.

benty *adj* covered in *bent* grass.

benweed *n* ragwort.

berry-heather *n* the crowberry.

besouth *adj, adv* to the southward of.

between-the-lights *n* twilight.

beuer *n* a beaver.

beust *n* grass two years old; grass withered from standing through the winter.

beusty *n* (applied to grass) dry and sapless, or somewhat withered.

bevir-horse *n* a lean horse, one worn-out with age or hard work.

bewest *adj*, *adv* to the west of.

beyont *prep*, *adv* beyond; at a great distance, as in "back-o' beyont".

bield *n*, *v* shelter, refuge, a home, anything that shelters or shades; a shelter of trees; to shelter; to protect; to take shelter.

biely *adj* affording shelter.

biettle, beetle *v* (applied to the vegetable kingdom) to recover, as in "the crap's beetlin' now".

big, bigg, begg *n* a particular species of barley, also denominated *bear*.

bilbie *n* a residence; a shelter.

bill, bill-blo, bill-jock *n* a bull.

billatory *n* a restless bull.

bindweed *n* ragwort.

bindwood *n* vulgar name for ivy.

bink *n* a hive; *bee-bink*, a nest or hive of bees; *wasp-bink*, a hive of wasps; a bank; an acclivity; the perpendicular part of a peat-moss, from which the labourer who stands opposite to it, cuts his peats, as in "bink of a peat-moss".

bing *n* a heap; a heap of grain; a pile of wood.

binkart *n* a pile of stones, dirt etc.

bird's-nest *n* wild carrot.

birley-oats *n* barley-oats; a species of oats.

birn *n*, *v* the high part of a farm where the young sheep are summered; dry, heathery pasture for summering lambs after weaning; a hill; to put lambs on a poor dry pasture; to burn.

birns *n* roots; the stronger stems of burnt heath, which remain after the smaller twigs are consumed.

birny *adj* covered with the scorched stems of heath that have been set on fire; (applied to plants) having a rough or stunted stem.

birs, birss *n* the gad-fly.

bizz *v* (applied to cattle) when, from being stung with the gadfly, they run madly about, as in "to take the bizz".

black-bides *n* bramble berries.

black crap *n* a crop of peas or beans; a name given to those crops which are always green, such as turnip, potatoes etc.

black-blutter *n* a blackberry, a bramble.

black-winter *n* the last cartload of grain brought in from the harvest field.

blackie *n* a kind of wild bee; a blackbird.

blaeberry *n* the bilberry.

blainy *adj* (applied to fields) frequent blanks in the crop, from the grain not having sprung up.

blair, blare *v, n* to make a noise, to cry loud; the bleat of a sheep.

blair *v* to become dry by exposure to the drout.

blairin *n* the ground on which flax is dried, or where peats are spread to dry.

blanded bear *n* barley and common bear mixed.

blander *v* to diffuse or disperse in a scanty and scattered way; (applied to seed-corn) said to be *blander'd* when very thinly sown.

blandish *n* the grain left uncut by careless reapers, generally in the furrows during a *kemp.*

blaver *n* the harebell; the corn bluebottle.

blawing-garss, -girss *n* blue mountain-grass, a herb, *Melica coerulea.*

blawort, blawart *n* the bluebottle; the round leaved bell-flower.

blemis *n* blossom, flowers.

blind man's ball, blind man's-bellows *n* the common puff-ball, or devil's snuff-box.

blood-tongue *n* the goose-grass.

bloom-fell *n* (perhaps) yellow clover.

bludie-bells *n* foxglove.

blue-blauers, -blaver *n* the plant called the bell-flower, or wild blue campanula.

bluefly *n* the fleshfly, or bluebottle.

bluidy-fingers *n* the foxglove.

bo-cow *n* a scarecrow; a bugbear.

bob, bobb *n* a tuft of grass growing above the rest.

bobantilter *n* an icicle.

bobbinqua *n* a quaking bog.

bochars and stars *n* the prickly-headed carex.

bockie *n* a bugbear.

bofft *adj* (used of standing grain) suffering from ravages of birds and from a long and wet harvest.

bog-nut *n* the marsh trefoil, *Menyanthes trifoliata.*

bogill, bogle *n* a scarecrow erected among growing potatoes; *potato-bogle.*

bomariskie *n* a herb, the roots of which taste exactly like licorice.

bonnage *n* an obligation, on the part of a tenant, to cut down the proprietor's corn.

bonnage-heuk *n* a tenant bound by the terms of his lease to reap, or use his hook, for the proprietor in harvest.

bonnage-peats *n* peats which, by his lease, a tenant is bound to furnish to the proprietor.

boo-lady *n* a cow.

boom *n, v* (used of a flying beetle) to make a booming sound.

boorick *n* a shepherd's hut.

bor, bourie *n* a small hole or crevice; a place used for shelter, especially by smaller animals.

bore *n* a crevice.

boroughmonger *n* a rabbit.

boss *adj* anything hollow.

bossins *n* vacancies in corn stacks for the admission of air to preserve the grain from being heated, from *boss*, hollow.

bothie *n* a cottage, often used to denote a place where labouring servants are lodged; it sometimes denotes a wooden hut.

bothne, bothene *n* a park in which cattle are fed and enclosed.

boucht *n* a small pen, usually put up in the corner of the fold, into which it was customary to drive the ewes when they were to be milked.

boucht *v* to enclose in a fold, properly ewes for milking.

bouchting-time *n* the time for milking ewes.

bourach *n* a small knoll, as distinguished from a brae; a shepherd's hut; a small heap of stones; a cluster, as of trees.

bousy, bowsie, bouzy *adj* bushy, wooded.

bout *n* the extent of ground mowed, while the labourer moves straight forward; the rectangle including the length of the field to be mowed, and the sweep of the scythe; corn or hay, when cut by the scythe, and lying in rows, is said to be "lying in the bout"; the act as going once round in ploughing.

boutgate *n* a circuitous road, a way which is not direct.

bow *n* the herd in general, whether enclosed in a fold or not; a fold for cows.

bowlochs *n* ragweed.

bowt *n* a thunderbolt.

box-drain *n* a drain in which the stones are carefully laid, so that there may be a regular opening for water.

bra, brae, bray *n* the side of a hill, an acclivity; the bank of a river; a hill.

brack *n* a strip of uncultivated ground between two *shots*, or plots of land.

brae-face *n* the front or slope of a hill.

brae-hag, brae-hauld *n* the

overhanging bank which has been undermined by a river.

brae-head *n* the summit of a hill.

brae-shot *n* a quantity of earth that has fallen from a steep slope.

brae-side *n* the declivity of a hill.

braeie, brayie *adj* sloping; hilly; declivous.

braid-band *adj, adv* corn laid out in the harvest field, on the band, but not bound, as in "lying in braid-band".

braidcast *v* sowing with the hand; (used of seed) scatter over the whole surface, broadcast.

brainding *v* striving to be first on the harvestfield.

braird *n* the first sprouting of grain.

brairdie *adj* abounding with sprouting grain.

brairds *n* the coarsest sort of flax.

brak-back, break-back *n* the harvest moon, so called, by the harvest labourers because of the additional work it entails.

brandur *n* a border.

brane *n* bran, the husks of corn ground.

brann, braun, brawn *n* a boar-pig.

brannie *n* a brindled cow.

brashloch *n* a crop of oats and rye, mixed, or of barley and rye.

bratchel *n* a heap of the husks of flax set on fire.

brath *v* to plait straw-ropes round a stack, crossing them at intervals.

braymen *n* the name given to those who inhabit the southern declivity of the Grampian hills.

breadth *n* a row of potatoes etc.

break *n* a division of land in a farm; a furrow in ploughing; a hollow in a hill.

break in *v* to go twice over the ground with the harrow; the first time that this implement is applied.

break-fur *n* rough ploughing.

breard *n* the first appearance of grain.

breck *n* barren ground in or near a town.

breckan *n* fern.

breckany *adj* full or covered with ferns, as in "breckany braes".

breer, brere, braird, breard *n* the first appearance of grain above-ground after it is sown.

breerie *adj* full of briars.

brick of land *phr* (perhaps) a division, a portion, as distinguished from others.

brig on a hair *phr* a very narrow bridge.

broakie *n* a cow with a black and white face.

broch *n* a prehistoric structure, in shape a circular tower, supposed to be Pictish; a halo round the sun or moon.

brock *n* a badger.

brock-holes *n* badger holes; dens or abodes of a badger.

brokittis *n* a red deer of two years old.

broo-lan' *n* steep ground.

broonie *n* a kind of wild bee.

brow *n* a steep hill or slope.

brown man of the muirs *phr, n* a *droich;* a dwarf, or subterranean elf.

brownie *n* a spirit, till of late years, supposed to haunt some old houses, those, especially, attached to farms. Instead of doing any injury he was believed to be very useful to the family, particularly to the servants, if they treated him well; for whom, while they took their necessary refreshment in sleep, he was wont to do many pieces of drudgery.

brumble *v* to make a hollow, mur-muring sound as rushing water.

brun *n* the brow of a hill.

bruntlin *n, adj* a burnt moor; of or belonging to a burnt moor; the blackbird; the corn bunting.

brym *n* border or margin of a river, lake or sea.

bu-kow *n* anything frightful as a scarecrow.

bucht, bught *n* a sheep or cattle-fold; a sheep-pen; a house for sheep at night; a square pew in a church.

buck-bean *n* the common trefoil.

buck-beard, buckbeard *n* the hard, whitish moss found growing on rocks, often in the shape of a wine-glass or inverted cone; a kind of whitish or grey lichen found growing on rocks on the edge of the woods, generally near water.

buckie-brier *n* the wild-rose.

buckie-faalie *n* the primrose.

bucky *n* the sluice of a mill-pond.

buft *adj* of standing corn, having the ears eaten by birds, or shaken by wind, or wasted by a prolonged harvest; shorn; half-shorn.

buggle *n* a bog, morass.

bughted-glade *n* a winding glade.

buind *n* a band of reapers or peat cutters.

bull *n* a dry sheltered place.

bull-head *n* a tadpole.

bull-segg, bulrush, bulwand *n* the common mugwort.

bum-clock *n* a humming, flying beetle, that flies in the summer evenings.

bum-pipe *n* the dandelion.

bumbee, bummer, bummie bee *n* a humble-bee, a wild bee that makes a great noise.

bumbee-byke *n* a nest of *bumbees*.

bumble-kite *n* a blackberry.

bummil, bummle, bombell *n* a wild bee.

bun *n* a rabbit; the tail of a rabbit.

bunnel *n* ragwort.

bunnerts *n* cow-parsnip, *Heracleum sphondylium.*

bunnle, bunewand, bunnelm bunnle, bunnerts *n* the cow-parsnip.

bunwede, bunweed, bund-weed *n* ragwort, a herb.

bur, bur-thrissel *n* the spear-thistle, *Carduus lanceolatus.*

burdocken *n* the burdock.

burian *n* a mound, a tumulus, or a kind of fortification.

burn *n* a brook; water from a fountain well.

burn-brae *n* the acclivity at the bottom of which a rivulet runs; a small rill running into a larger stream.

burnside *n* the ground situated on the side of a rivulet.

burran *n* a badger.

burrel ley *n* land, where at mid-summer there was only a narrow ridge ploughed, and a large strip or baulk of barren land, between every ridge.

bursen-kirn *n* such a laborious harvest that all the grain is not cut before sunset.

bush *v* to place bushes on fields to prevent poachers from netting partridges.

bushel *n* a small dam.

busk *n* a bush.

buss *n* a thicket; a clump or stand of trees; a wood; a bush; a small ledge of rocks projecting into the sea, covered with seaweed.

bussie *adj* bushy.

butt *n* a piece of ground, which in ploughing does not form a proper ridge, but is excluded as an angle; a small piece of ground disjoined from the adjacent lands.

butt-rig *n* a ridge.

buttery *n* a butterfly.

buttle *n* a sheaf; a bundle of hay or straw.

button-mouse *n* a small field-mouse.

by *adv, prep* beyond.

byking *n* a hive, a swarm.

C

ca, caw *n* a pass or defile between hills.

cabbage-fauld *n* a place where cabbage is grown.

cair, cayr *v* to return to a place where one has been before.

cairn *n* a heap of stones thrown together in a conical form.

cairny *adj* abounding with *cairns*, or heaps of stones.

calf-country, calf-ground, caufgrun *n* one's native place; the place of one's nativity, or where one has been brought up.

calf, calf-sod *n* the sod or sward bearing fine grass, (perhaps) as affording excellent food for rearing calves; "crop and calf", crop and grass.

calflea *n* infield ground, one year under natural grass, probably thus denominated from the calves being fed on it.

calver *n* a cow with calf.

cambie leaf *n* the water lily.

came *n* a honeycomb.

camp *n* an oblong heap of potatoes earthed up for being kept through winter.

cancer *n* the red campion; the burying beetle.

canch *n* a breadth of digging land.

canna-down *n* the cotton-grass. see also *cats tails*.

canny nannie *n* a kind of bumble-bee.

cant *n* a little rise of rocky ground on a highway.

cant-robin *n* the dwarf wild-rose, with white flowers.

capyl *n* a horse or mare.

capper *n* a spider.

carameil, carameile, carmele, carmylie *n* heath peas, an edible root, *Orobus tuberosus*.

carl-doddie *n* a stalk of rib-grass that bears the flowers.

carlin-heather *n* fine-leaved heath, *Erica cinerea*.

carlin-spurs *n* needle spurs, or petty whin, *Genista anglica*.

carn-tangle *n* the large, long fucus, with roots not unlike those of a tree, cast ashore on the beach after a storm at sea.

carr-gate *n* a road across steep rocks.

carse *n* the watercress; a stretch of low, fertile land near a river.

casting *n, v* (applied to bees) the act of swarming; land on which crops fail to ripen.

catcluke *n* trefoil; a herb, *Lotus corniculatus*, named for some fanciful resemblance it has to a cat or a bird's foot.

cat heather *n* a finer species of heath, low and slender, growing more in separate upright stalks than the common heath, and flowering only at the top.

catchrogue *n* cleavers or goose-grass; a herb generally growing in hedges, and adhering to the clothes of those who attempt to break through them, *Galium aparine*.

cats-tails *n* hare's-tail-tush; cotton grass, *Eriophorum vaginatum*.

catten-clover, cat-in-clover *n* the lotus; bird's foot trefoil.

cattle-creep *n* a low arch or gangway to enable cattle to pass under or over a railway.

cattle-raik *n* a common or extensive pasture where cows graze at large.

caul, cauld *v* "to caul the banks of a river", to lay a bed of loose stones from the channel of the river backwards, as far as may be necessary, for defending the land against the inroads of the water; a damhead; a weir on a river to divert water into a mill-lade.

cauld-yird *n* the grave.

causey *n* a street.

Charlewan, Charlewayne *n* the constellation *Ursa Major*, also called the Plough.

chasbol, chesbol, chesbow *n* the poppy.

chickenwort *n* chickweed, *Alsine media*.

choop *n* the fruit of the wild briar, *Rubus major*.

chuckie-stane *n* a small pebble; a quartz crystal rounded by attrition on the beach.

clachan, claghan, clauchanne *n* a small village bordering the Highlands in which there is a parish church.

claddach, cleddach *n* a shingly beach.

clattermalloch *n* meadow trefoil.

claver *n* clover.

cleddiwig *n* a stone quarry.

cleg *n* a gad-fly; a horse-fly.

clet *n* a rock or cliff in the sea, broken off from the adjoining rocks on the shore.

cleuch, cleugh *n* a precipice; a rugged ascent; a straight hollow between precipitous banks or a hollow descent on the side of a hill.

cleuch-brae *n* a cliff overhanging a ravine.

clevis *n* clover.

clewch *n* a hollow between steep banks, a narrow glen or valley; also, a precipice, high rocky bank; cliffs, shelving rocks; also gaps or glens between rocks.

clift *n* a cliff; high and steep rock; a steep rocky hillside.

clint *n* a hard or flinty rock; crevices amongst bare limestone rocks; any pretty large stone, of a hard kind.

clinted *adj* (used of sheep), caught among cliffs by leaping down to a ledge from which ascent is impossible by leaping back.

clinty *adj* stony.

clippart, clippie *n* a shorn sheep.

clock-bee *n* a species of beetle.

clockleddie *n* the ladybird.

clodder *n* the person who throws up peats to the builder of the stack.

cloddoch *n* a small heap of stones.

cloddy *adj* full of clods.

cloff *n* a fissure of any kind; a cleft between adjacent hills.

cloich *n* a place of shelter; the cavity of a rock where one may elude a search.

clootie's-craft *n* the devil's croft; a small portion of land set apart for

the devil, and left untilled.

clouse, clowse *n* a sluice; a ditch.

clowe *n* a hollow between hills.

clowns *n* butterwort, a herb, also called sheep-rot.

cluddock *n* a dry, shingly bed at the side of a stream.

co *n* a rock-cave, with a narrow entrance, on the seashore.

cock's-caim *n* meadow pinks, or cuckoo flower, *Lychnis flos cuculi*.

cock-head *n* the herb all heal, *Stachys palustris*.

cockiloorie *n* a daisy.

cockrose *n* any wild poppy with a red flower.

codgebell *n* an earwig.

coilheuch *n* a coal pit.

cole *n* a haycock.

collinhood *n* the wild poppy.

colpindach *n* a young cow who has never calved.

come *n* growth; the act of vegetation, there's a considerable degree of vegetation, as in "there's a come in the grund".

come-o'-will *n* a herb, shrub or tree, that springs up spontaneously, not having been planted; hence applied to any animal that comes of its own accord into one's possession; transferred to new settlers in a country or district, who can show no ancient standing there; (perhaps) a bastard child.

con *n* the squirrel.

contrimont *adv* against the hill; upwards.

cooie, cowie *n* a small cow; a hornless cow.

coomb *n* the bosom of a hill having a semicircular form; a hollow in a mountain.

coop *n* a small heap, a heap of dung, as in "a coop o' muck".

cooser *n* a stallion.

corbie-aits *n* a species of black oats, denominated, (perhaps) from their black colour.

corf *n* a temporary building, a shed.

corf-house *n* a house, a shed, erected for the purpose of curing salmon, and for keeping the nets in.

corkes *n* the ancient name for the *Lichen omphalodes*, now in Scotland called Cudbear, *Lichen tartareus.*

corkir *n* the *Lecanora tartarea* of the Highlands and Isles.

corn-loft *n* a granary.

corny *adj* fruitful or plentiful in grain, as in "the last was a corny year".

corrie *n* a hollow between hills, or rather, in a hill.

coster *n* a piece of arable land.

cottar *n* one who inhabits a *cot*, or cottage, dependent on a farm.

cottar-wark *n* stipulated work done by cottagers to the farmer on whose land they dwell.

cotter *v* to get a piece of ground free of rent for one year, to raise potatoes; the manure and culture being considered an equivalent for the use of the ground.

cottown *n* a small village, or hamlet, possessed by *cottars*, or cottagers, dependent on the principal farm.

covan *n* a convent.

couhirt *n* a cow-herd.

country-side *n* the common term with the vulgar, in Scotland, for a district or tract of country.

coutch *n* a portion of land lying in one division, in contradistinction from that which is possessed in *runrig*

coutch *v* (applied to land in regard to a proper and convenient division among joint proprietors or possessors) to lay out, or lay down.

coutch be cawill *phr* to divide lands, as properly laid together, by lot.

cove *n* a cave.

covin-tree *n* a large tree in front of an old Scottish mansion-house where the laird always met his visitors.

cow *n* a scarecrow, hence the compound word *worrie-cow*; a hobgoblin.

cow-cakes *n* wild parsnip, *Heracleum sphondylium*.

cow-cloos *n* common trefoil, *Trifolium pretense*.

cow-grass *n* a species of clover; common purple clover.

cow-heave *n* the herb *Tussilago*, (perhaps) originally cow-hoof, from a supposed resemblance to the hoof of a cow.

cowmack *n* a herb supposed to have great virtue in making the cow desire the male.

cowpendoch *n* a young cow.

cow-quake *n* an affection of cattle, caused by the chillness of the weather.

cowslem *n* an ancient name given to the evening star.

craft *n* croft; a piece of land adjoining a house.

craid, croyd *n* perhaps yellow clover.

craig *n* a rock; a crag; a rocky place.

craiglugge *n* the point of a rock.

craigy *adj* rocky.

craik *n* the landrail; to carry on courtship by night, under the canopy of heaven, as in "to listen to the craik in the corn".

crap-land *n* land under crop.

crap o' the causey *phr* the crown or raised middle of the causeway.

craw-bogie, craw-deil *n* the scarecrow.

craw-day *adv, n* the morning; dawn.

craw-croops *n* crowberries.

craw-flower, craw-tae *n* the wild hyacinth, *ranunculus*.

creech *n* a declivity encumbered with large stones.

creek o' day *adv, n, phr* daybreak.

creeping-bur *n* the club-moss.

creeping-seefer *n* the ivy-leaved toad-flax.

creeping-wheat-grass *n* couch-grass.

crisp, crispe *n* a cobweb lawn.

croft *n* a crop; a small piece of land left untilled, and dedicated to the devil, as in "the goodman's croft".

crony *n* a potato.

crony-hill *n* a potato field.

crooks *n* the windings of a river.

croon, croun, crune *n, v* (used of cattle) to low; to roar in a menacing tone like an angry bull.

crottlie *adj* covered with lichen.

croydie *n* a *croydie lea* is a field on which there is a great quantity of foggage for sheltering game.

crue *n* a sheep pen or smaller fold.

crufe *n* a pen for cattle; a pigsty; a hovel.

crukis *n* the windings of a river, hence it came to signify the space of ground closed in on one side by these windings, as The Crook of Devon.

cuddie *n* a gutter on a street; an ass.

cuddoch, cuddock *n* a young cow; a heifer.

cuisser, cursour, cusser *n* a stallion.

cultie *n* a young colt; a nimble-footed animal.

cumlin *n* an animal that comes and attaches itself voluntarily to a person or place.

cuning *n* a rabbit.

cuningar *n* a rabbit-warren.

cup-moss *n* a name given to the lichen *Tartareus.* The name probably originates from the resemblance of the fructification to *cups*.

cuppo *n* a hollow place.

curl-doddie *n* the cone of a pine- or fir tree; curled cabbage ; natural clover ; ribgrass

curlie-doddie *n* the scabious, or devil's bit, *Scabiosa arvensis.*

curlies *n* colewort, of which the leaves are curled.

curluns *n* the earth-nut; the pig-nut, *Bunium bulbocastanum.*

curran-petris *n* the name given to a certain root, the wild carrot.

cuthil *n* corn carried to another field than that on which it grew.

cutle *v* to carry corn out of water-mark to higher ground or from low to high ground that it may be sooner dried, as in "to cutle corn"; from a damp to a dry position with the same view, from a *lown* or a sheltered spot to one that is exposed to the wild. The same term is used when corn is removed from a distant part of the field, or of the farm, to one that is nearer, so that, when ready to be stacked, or housed, it may not be necessary to fetch it far in bad roads.

cutle *n* the corn set up in this manner. It is sometimes removed to give liberty to the cattle to eat the foggage.

cuttie *n* a hare.

cuttie-clap *n* the couch of a hare; its seat or lair.

cuttie's fud *n* a hare's tail.

D

daighie *adj* (applied to rich ground) composed of clay and sand in due proportions.

dail *n* a field.

dair away *v* (used of sheep) to wander, roam from their usual pasture.

dale-land *n* the lower and arable ground of a district.

dalloch *n* a flat piece of rich land.

dallop *n* a steep shank or glen, where two haughs are exactly opposite each other.

damsched *n* a portion of land bordering on a dam.

dank-will *n* a will o' the wisp.

darkening *n* evening, twilight.

daugh *n* a certain division of land, determined by its being able to produce forty-eight bolls.

dauk *adj* dark, murky.

dawache, davoch, davach *n* a considerable tract of land; a small district, including several ox-gangs; an ancient measure of land.

dawaytt *n* a thin flat turf.

dawing *n* dawn of day.

day-nettles *n* dead nettles, a herb, *Lamium album.*

dayligaun *n* the twilight.

day-sky *n* the appearance of the sky at break of day or at twilight.

dead men's bells *n* the purple foxglove.

dead ripe *adj, adv* so ripe that all growth has ceased.

dead-lown *adj* completely still; (applied to the atmosphere) a dead calm.

dead-thraw *n* the last agonies of expiring nature.

deadman's-sneechin *n* the dust of the common puff-ball.

deal, dealle *n* a division of land, a distinct portion.

dean *n* a hollow where the ground slopes on both sides; a deep wooded valley; a small valley.

dearth-cap *n* a species of fungus which in its form resembles a bowl, or what in Scotland is called a *cap*, containing a number of seeds.

dede time o' the year, dead time o' the year *phr* midwinter, when there is no vegetation.

dede-man's-sneezin *n* the dust of the common puffball. The idea mentioned by Linnaeus, as prevailing in Sweden, that the dust of this plant caused blindness, is also prevalent in this country.

deer-hair, deers-hair *n* heath club-rush, a coarse species of pointed grass, which in May bears a very minute but beautiful yellow flower.

deil-in-a-bush *n* love-in-the-mist, *Nigella damascene,* the herb paris.

deil's apple-rennie *n* the wild chamomile.

deil's apple-trees *n* the sun spurge.

deil's barley *n* the crimson stone-crop.

deil's-bit *n* the *Scabiosa succisa,* a herb, so denominated because it seems to have a bit or bite taken off the root, which by the vulgar is said to have been done by the devil.

deil's beef-tub *n* a roaring linn.

deil's butterfly *n* the tortoise-shell butterfly.

deil's darning needle *n* the dragonfly; the shepherd's needle.

deil's dung *n* asafoetida, named for its stench.

deil's snuffbox *n* the common puff-ball.

deil's spaderfu's *n* natural heaps or hummocks of sand or gravel.

deil's specs *n* cup-and-ring marks.

deil's spoons *n* the water plantain; the broadleafed bindweed.

deir, dere *n* a wild animal, or any wild beast of game.

deisheal *adv, n* with the sun, from east to west.

dello *n* a small patch of cultivated land.

den *n* a glen, dell, ravine.

dentilion, dentilioun *n* the dandelion.

dere *n* a deer, or any wild beast of game.

derkening *n* the evening twilight.

deuk *n* covert; shelter.

deule weeds *n* mourning weeds.

devaill *n* an inclined plane for a waterfall; a descent; a fall in ground.

dew-cup *n* the herb called ladies mantle, *Alchemilla vulgaris.*

dighter *n* one who is employed in winnowing grain.

dike *n* a wall.

dim *n* midnight, as in "the head of the dim"; midsummer twilight between sunset and sunrise.

dippen *n* the stairs at a river side, (perhaps) steps for dipping, or the place where women *dip* their buckets to bring up water.

dirt-flee *n* the yellow fly that haunts dung hills.

divise *n* a term denoting the boundary by which land is divided; also a portion of land, as defined by its boundaries.

dog's lugs *n* fox-glove, or *Digitalis*, probably denominated from the resemblance of the leaves to the ears of a dog.

dog's sillar *n* yellow rattle or cock's comb.

doggie-hillag *n* a small hillock with long grass.

doit *n* a name sometimes given to a kind of rye-grass.

donie *n* a hare.

doolloup, doulloup *n* a steep *shank*, or glen, where two *haugh*s are exactly opposite each other; a sloping hollow between two hills.

doon-brae *adv* downwards.

doon-lie *n* a grave; a resting place.

dounsetting *adj* the setting of the sun.

dounthrough *adv* in the low or flat country, as in "I'm gaun down-through", I am going to the lower part of the country, and "he bides dounthrough", he resides in the lower part.

dour-seed *n* the name given to a late species of oats, from its tardiness in ripening.

dovatt *n* a thin turf.

dove-dock *n* the coltsfoot.

downans *n* green hillocks.

downfall, downfa' *n* a declivity in ground; a slope; the practice of allowing the sheep to descend from the hills in winter to the lower lands lying contiguous, as in "winter downfall".

dratsie *n* the common otter.

drave *n* a drove of cattle.

drawling *n* bog cotton or moss-crop, a plant.

drizzen *v* to low as a cow or ox, sometimes applied to a sluggard groaning over his work.

drucht *n* drought, a season of drought.

drum *n* a knoll; a ridge; applied to little hills, which rise as ridges above the level of adjacent ground.

drumlie-droits *n* bramble-berries.

drune *n* the murmuring sound emitted by cattle.

dry-dyke, dry-stane-dyke *n* a stone wall built without lime.

dry-gair-flow *n* the place where two hills join and form a kind of bosom.

dule *n* a boundary of land.

dun *n* a hill; eminence.

dustie-melder *n* the designation

given to the last quantity of grain sent, for the season, by a farmer to the mill.

dustie-miller *n* the plant *Auricula*, so denominated from the leaves being covered in a whitish dust.

dwaming *v* the fading of light.

dyke *n* a wall.

dyke-louper *n* a beast that transgresses all fences.

dyke-loupin' *n* primarily applied to cattle, that cannot be kept within walls or fences; transferred to loose or immoral conduct.

dykie *n* a small or low wall.

dyne *n* a dale.

DRUMLIE-DROITS

E

each *n* a horse.

ear *v* to plough or till land.

eard *n* earth; unploughed land.

eard-bark *n* the roots of the tormentil, used for tanning.

eard-din *n* thunder; an earthquake.

eard-fast *adj* deep rooted in the earth; a stone or boulder fixed firmly in the earth.

earning-grass *n* common

butterwort.

earthins *adj, adv* earthwards, along the ground.

easel, east-bye, eastit *adj, adv, n* eastward.

eastning-wort *n* the scabious, a plant.

ebb-land *n* shallow soil.

echer *n* an ear of corn.

edge *n* the highest part of a mooring and elevated tract of ground, of considerable extent, generally that which lies between two streams; a kind of ridge.

eel-backit *adj* (applied to a dun-coloured horse) having a black line on the back.

eebrek crap *n* the third crop after lea.

eetnoch *n* a moss-grown, precipitous rock.

elbowit grass *n* flote foxtail-grass, *Alopecurus geniculatus*, denominated *elbowit*, or *elbowed*, for the same reason for which it bears the name of *Geniculatus*, as being *kneed*, or having many joints.

eldin-docken *n* *Rumex aquaticus*, the water-dock, found by the sides of rivers, often cut, dried and used as *eldin*, or fuel, by the lower classes, thence supposed to have its name.

elements *n* the sky; the firmament; the heavens.

elf-cup *n* the name given to small stones perforated by friction at a waterfall and believed to be the workmanship of the elves.

ellwand of stars *phr* the three stars in the northern constellation of Lyra; the King's or Lady's Ellwand, the stars of Orion's Belt.

emmock, enanteen *n* a pismire; an ant.

endlangin *v* harrowing a field along the furrows.

erchin *n* a hedgehog.

ern-fern *n* the brittle fern, "the eagle fern".

ernit *n* the pig-nut.

etnagh *adj* of or belonging to juniper.

ettercap *n* a spider.

ever, iver *adj* (applied to places where there are two of the same name) denoting that which is uppermost, or further up the hill, reckoning from the bed of the nearest river.

everocks *n* the cloudberry, knout-berry, *Rubus chamaemorus*.

ew-gowan *n* common daisy.

ewie *n* a young ewe; a small fir-cone.

F

fa' awalt *v* to fall without the power of getting up again; (originally applied to sheep) hence to a person intoxicated and the phrase, "to roll awald".

faboris *n* suburbs.

fade *n* a company of hunters.

fail, fale, feal *n* any grassy part of the surface of the ground.

fail-dyke *n* a wall built of sods; a wall of turf.

fain *adj* damp; (applied to grain in the field) not thoroughly dry, not fit for being taken in.

faintie grund *n* ground in the course of a journey or excursion, on which, when one passes over it, the superstitious believe it to be necessary to have a bit of bread in one's pocket, in order to prevent the person from fainting.

fair-grass *n* bulbous crowfoot, or butter-cups, *Ranunculus bulbosus*, said to be denominated from the whiteness of the under part of the leaf.

fairy green *n* a small circle, often observed on old *leas* or heath, of a deeper green than the surrounding sward, supposed by the vulgar or superstitious to be the spot on which the fairies hold their dances.

fairy-hillocks *n* verdant knolls, denominated from the vulgar idea that these were anciently inhabited by the fairies, or that they used to dance there.

fairy rade *n* the designation given to the expedition made by the fairies to the place in which they are to hold their great annual banquet on the first of May.

fald, fauld *n* a sheep-fold; a enclosure of any kind.

fald-dike *n* a wall of turf, surrounding the space appropriated for a fold.

fale *n* turf.

fallen stars *n* jelly tremella, *Tremella nostoc*, a gelatinous plant, found in pastures after rain.

fallow-break *n* land under grass for two years and then ploughed up.

fank *n* a sheep-cot or pen.

far-hie-an-antour *adv* at a considerable distance.

farres *n* boundaries; ridges marked out by the plough.

far yaud *n* the cry made by a shepherd to his dog, when he is to drive away some sheep at a distance.

fastan reid deare *n* deer of a deep red colour.

fauch, faugh *adj, n, v* fallow, not sowed; a single furrow, from *lea*; to fallow ground.

fauchs *n* a division of a farm, so called because it gets no manuring, but is prepared for a crop by a slight fallowing.

faulds *n* a division of a farm, so denominated because it is manured by folding sheep and other cattle upon it.

fauxburghe *n* a suburb.

fawn *n* a white spot on moorish and mossy ground.

fe, fee, fey, fie *n* cattle; small cattle, sheep or goats; possessions in general; wages; hereditary property in land.

feedle *n* a field.

feedlie *n* a small field.

feer *v* to draw the first furrow in ploughing; to mark out the riggs before ploughing the whole field.

feitho, fethok *n* a polecat.

fell *n* a wild and rocky hill; high land only fit for pasture.

fell-bloom *n* the flower of the *Lotus corniculatus*, or bird's-foot trefoil.

fellin-grass *n* the plant called

angelica.

felt *n* creeping wheatgrass; couch-grass; a thick growth of weeds; the missel-thrush.

fen *n* mud; filth.

fern-seed *n* to render one's self invisible by means of this seed, or the mode of gathering it, as a charm, as in "to gather the fern seed".

ferny-buss *n* a clump of ferns; a bush or fern; as in "it's either a tod or a ferny-buss", it's something or other, no matter what.

ferny-hirst *n* a hill-side covered with ferns.

ferrekyn *n* a firkin.

feure *n* furrow.

feverfoullie *n* feverfew.

fey *n* croft or *infield* land.

fey-crop *n* a crop more than usually good, portending the owner's death.

fiedle *n* a field.

fieldert, fieldwart *prep, adv* towards the fields; abroad.

fier *v* to mark out ridges with a plough.

filsch, filch *n* weeds or grass covering the ground, especially when under crop.

filschy *adj* applied to a sheaf when swelled up with weeds or natural grass.

fiold *n* a hill; upland pasturage.

fintock *n* the cloudberry or knout-berry, *Rubus chamaemorus*, otherwise called *averin*.

finzach *n* knot-grass, *Polygonum aviculare.*

firth *n* a place on the moor where peats for fuel could be cut; a small wood.

fit-stool *n* the face of the earth, God's footstool.

fitch *v* to move anything a little way from its former place; to make a slight change in a situation of a landmark, as in "to fitch a march-stane".

fittings *n* turf set on edge, two by two, for the purpose of drying.

flaa *n* a thin turf.

flat *n* a field.

flauch o' land *n* a division of land.

flaucht o' land *n* a croft.

flauchter *v* to pare turf from the ground.

flauchter-fail *n* a long turf cut with a flaughter spade.

flaver *n* grey-bearded oats, *Avena fatua.*

flaw *n* an extent of land under grass; a broad ridge; the spot of ground occupied by an individual, on the edge of a moss, on which his

peats are spread for being dried, in the summer season, as in "a flaw of peats".

flaw-peat *n* a soft and spongy peat.

fleaks *n* the fissures between the strata of a rock.

fleeing-adder, -dragon *n* a dragon-fly.

fleeing-buss *n* a whin bush on fire.

fleet-dyke *n* a dike erected for preventing inundation.

float *n* the strip of a ploughed field between two open furrows, three poles or so in breadth.

flock-raik *n* a range of pasture for a flock of sheep.

floe *n* a bog; a morass.

floss *n* the common rush.

flot *n* part of land ploughed at one turn, usually four rigs.

flourish *n* blossom.

flow *n* a watery moss; a low-lying piece of rough, watery land, not broken up.

flush *n* a piece of moist ground; a place where water frequently lies; a morass.

flutter-baw *n* the puff-ball.

flyam *n* a large seaweed tangle, growing round the shore.

fog, fug *n, v* moss; to become

covered in moss.

fog-clad *adj* moss-covered.

foggage *n* rank grass which has not been eaten in summer, or which grows among grain, and is fed on by horses or cattle after the crop is removed.

foggie, foggy, foggit, fuggy *adj* mossy.

foggie, foggie-bee *n* a small yellow bee, that builds her cells among the *fog* or moss; a kind of humble bee.

fool's-parsley *n* the lesser hemlock.

fool's-stones *n* the male and female orchis, *Orchis morio*.

foose *n* the house-leek.

forenicht *adv, n* the early part of the night; the interval between twilight and bedtime.

forthens *adv, adj* at a distance.

fossa *n* grass growing among stubble.

fouat, fow, fouse *n* the house-leek.

fow *n* a mop or heap of corn in the sheafs, or of bottles of straw after being thrashed.

fowmarte *n* a polecat.

foxterleaves *n* the fox-glove.

foynie, funyie *n* the wood-marten, or beech-marten.

frandie *n* a hay-cock; a small rick of sheaves such as a man, standing on the ground, can build.

free-coup *n* a place for emptying rubbish.

French-butterfly *n* the common white butterfly.

French-puppy *n* the eastern poppy.

fricht-the-craw *n* a scarecrow.

frunter *n* a ewe in her fourth year.

fuddie *n* a hare.

fumart, funyle *n* the polecat.

furrow cow *n* a cow that is not with calf.

futrat, futteret *n* a weasel.

FRANDIES

G

ga-fur *n* a furrow for a run of water.

gaber *n* a lean horse.

gad *n* a large mass of ice.

gaffol-land *n* land liable to taxation; also denoting land rented.

gair, gare *n* a slip of tender fertile grass in a barren situation.

gail, gail-bush *n* the bog myrtle.

gairy *n* a steep hill or precipice; moorland; a piece of wasteland.

gaiter-tree *n* an old name given to the bramble.

gaitin *n* a setting up of sheaves singly on their ends to dry.

gallbushes *n* a shrub which grows plentifully in wild moorland marshes, the scent of it is extremely strong.

gallion *n* a lean horse.

galloway-dyke *n* a wall built firmly at the bottom but no thicker at the top than the length of the single stones, loosely piled the one above the other.

garnel *n* a granary, corn-chest.

garron *n* a small horse; an old stiff horse; a tall, stout fellow.

garten berries *n* bramble berries.

garwhoungle *n* the noise of the bittern in rising from the bog.

gaskins *n* the name commonly given to a rough green gooseberry, originally brought from *Gascony.*

gateless *adj* pathless.

gaw *n* a channel or furrow for drawing off water; a hollow with water-springs in it.

gean, geen *n* the wild cherry.

geit *n* a fence or border.

gell *adj* (used of animals) barren; (used of cows) not giving milk.

gelloch *n* an earwig.

geo *n* a deep hollow; a creek or chasm in the shore.

gerslouper *n* a grasshopper.

gersy *adj* grassy.

gerss-house *n* a house possessed by a tenant who has no land attached to it.

gewlich *n* an earwig.

gibloan *n* a muddy loan, or miry path, which is so soft that one cannot walk on it.

gil, gill *n* a cavern; a steep narrow

A *Scots* Dictionary *of Nature*

glen; a ravine: it is generally applied to a gully whose sides have resumed a verdant appearance in consequence of the grass growing; the bed of a mountain torrent.

gill *n* a leech.

gill-ronie *n* a ravine abounding with brushwood.

gill-gatherer *n* one who gathers leeches in the marshes.

gimmer-pet *n* a ewe that is two years old.

gio *n* a deep ravine which admits the sea.

girsing *n* the place for cutting *feals* or *turfs*, and for grazing cattle.

girst *n* pastured on grass.

girthgate *n* a safe road; the way to a sanctuary.

glack *n* a defile between mountains; a ravine in a mountain; an opening in a wood where the wind comes with force; a narrow glen.

glair *n* mud.

glair-hole *n* a mire.

glar, glaur *n* mud, mire.

glen *n* a daffodil.

gloam *v* twilight comes on, as in "it gloams".

gloamin, gloaming-fa' *n, adv* evening; twilight.

gloaming-shot *n* a twilight interval which workmen within doors take before using lights

gloamin-star *n* the evening star.

gloam't *adj* in the state of twilight.

glupe *n* a great chasm or cavern.

go-harvest, go-har'st *n* the fall, when the season declines or is about to go away; including the time from the ingathering of the crop till the commencement of winter.

good neighbours *phr, n* a title given to the fairies; a flattering designation formerly given to witches.

gool *n* corn marigold.

goose-corn *n* field brome-grass.

gords *n* land now waste, that had formerly been cultivated.

goresta *n* the boundary of a ridge of land.

gorsk, gosk *n* strong rank grass.

gowan *n* the generic name for the daisy; *ewe-gowan,* the common daisy, probably from the ewe, as being frequent in pastures and fed on by sheep; *horse-gowan,* the *Leontodon,* the *Hypochaeris* and the *Crepis; large white gowen,* the ox-eye; *lucken-gowan,* the globe-flower; *witch-gowan,* witch-gowan flowers are large yellow gowans with a stalk filled with pernicious sap, resembling milk, and called by the peasantry "witches' milk"; *yellow-gowan,* denoting different species of the *Ranunculus,* the marsh marigold, and corn marigold.

gowan'd *adj* covered with the mountain daisy.

gowan-shank *n* the stalk of a mountain-daisy.

gowan-sparkled, -speckled *adj* sprinkled with daisies.

gowany *adj* abounding with daisies.

gowk-bear *n* great golden maiden hair.

gowk's host *n* Canterbury bells, wild hyacinth.

gowk's meat *n* wood sorrel.

gowk's shillings *n* yellow rattle.

gowk's spittle *n* the frothy matter frequently seen on the leaves of plants.

gowl *n* a hollow between hills; the opening between the sides of a shock of corn, as in "the gowl o' the crook".

graff *n* a ditch, trench, or foss.

grain *n* a branch of a river; the branches of a valley at the upper end, where it divides into two.

gramshoch *adj* (applied to the growth of grain, vegetables etc) coarse, rank.

Granzebene *n* the Grampian mountains.

grass-meal *n* the grass that will keep a cow for a season.

grave *n* a grove.

gray *n* twilight.

gray geese *n* a name vulgarly given to large field stones lying on the surface of the ground.

green-kail-worm *n* a caterpillar.

grey *n* a badger.

grey o' the morning *phr* dawn of day.

greking, gryking *n* peep of day.

grimes-dike *n* a ditch made by magic.

gristy *n* a strip of grass between ridges of corn.

grool *n* a kind of moss beat into peat.

grose, groser, groset, grosse, grossart, grosset *n* a gooseberry.

grosset-buss *n* a gooseberry-bush.

ground-rotten, grund-rotten *n* the brown rat.

groundie swallow *n* groundsel.

growthiness *n* the state of strong vegetation or luxuriance.

grozart, grozel, grozer, grozet, grozzle *n* a gooseberry.

grull *n* a stone ground to dust.

grummel *n* mud.

grunye *n* a promontory.

grushie *adj* of thriving growth;

thick.

guids *n* cattle, livestock.

guild, guilde *n* corn marigold.

guilder-faugh *n* old *lea-land*, once ploughed and allowed to lie fallow.

gule *n* corn marigold.

gulghy *n* a beetle; a cockchafer.

gulliewillie *n* a quagmire covered with grass.

gullion *n* a quagmire; mud.

gushing *v, n* the grunting of a pig.

gutter *n* a mire, as in "the road was a perfect gutter".

gyll *n* a glen.

gyre-carling *n* Hecate, or the mother-witch of the peasants; a hob-goblin; a scarecrow.

gyte, gytt *n* a small sheaf of corn set by itself to dry in a field.

gytlin *adj* rural, belonging to the fields.

H

---

ha' *n* low-lying land beside a stream.

ha'-rig *n* a ridge; the first ridge in a harvest field; thus denominated because it is cut down by the domestics on the farm, i.e. the members of the farmer's family. It is deemed the post of honour. The other reapers are understood to keep always a little behind those who have this more honourable station, which is therefore also called the *foremost rig*.

habitackle *n* habitation.

haches *n* racks for hay.

hack *n* a wild moorish place; a *hag*.

hackit *adj* (used of animals) white-faced.

hackit-flesh *n* a charm of carrion for injuring a neighbour's live-stock.

had *n* a holding; a house; a den; an animal's lair; a place of retreat or concealment.

haen *v* to preserve land for hay etc.

haerst, hairst, haist, hearst *n, v* harvest.

haft *n, v* usual pasture; a domicile; a haunt; to accustom sheep or cattle to a new pasture.

hag, hagg *n* wild, broken ground; a piece of soft bog in a moor; a hole in a moss from which peats have been cut; a water-hollow, wet in winter and dry in summer; an islet of grass in the midst of a bog.

hag-stane *n* a boundary stone.

hah-yaud *n* a shepherd's call to his dog to make a wide sweep round the flock he is driving.

haigh *n* a steep bank; a precipice; a *heuch.*

hain *v* to enclose; to defend by a hedge, (as applied to grass) to preserve from being cut down or pastured.

hair *n* the last pickle corn to be cut on a farm.

hair-stane *n* boundary-stone.

hairst, haist *n* the harvest.

hairst-day *n* a day during harvest.

hairst-folks *n* harvesters.

hairst-hog *n* a sheep smeared at the end of harvest, when it ceases to be a lamb.

hairst-home *n* winter.

hairst-maiden *n* a figure formed of a sheaf, surmounting the last load of corn brought home.

hairst-mune, -meen *n* harvest moon; the designation given to the moon during her autumnal aspect, when she appears larger than at other seasons.

hairst-play *n* the school holidays during harvest.

hairst-rig *n* the field on which reaping goes on, as in "will ye gang out and see the hairst-rig?".

hairy-brotag, -cobit, -cubit *n* any large, hairy caterpillar.

hallior *n* a term applied to the moon in her last quarter, when much in the wane.

hame *n* home

hamegain', home-going *n* the act of going home or returning to one's own habitation. Thus it is said ironically, when one meets with something very disagreeable on one's return, "I got a bonny walcom for my hamegain".

hamesucken *adj* greatly attached to one's home.

hammel *n* an open shed for sheltering cattle; a stage on posts to support hay, corn etc.

haning, haining *n* hedges, enclo-sures; any field where the grass or crop is protected from being eaten up, or destroyed, whether enclosed or not.

happen *n* the path trodden by cattle, especially on high ground.

happergraw *n, v* a blank in growing corns, caused by unequal sowing; to sow grain unequally, in consequence of which it springs up in patches.

happergraw *n* a blank in growing corns, caused by unequal sowing.

hard-head *n* sneezewort, *Achillea ptarmica*.

harrow-slaying *n, v* a term used to denote the destruction of grass seeds by rain, before they have struck root, when the mould has been too much pulverized.

haryage, hairyche *n* a collective word applied to horses or cattle.

hass of a hill *n* a defile; the throat or narrow passage.

haugh, hawch, hauch, halche *n* low lying flat ground, properly on the border of a river, and such as is sometimes over-flowed.

haugh-ground *n* low-lying land.

haughland *n* of or belonging to low-lying ground.

hay-bog *n* a damp hay-meadow.

hazel-shaw *n* an abrupt, flat piece of ground at the bottom of a hill, covered with hazels.

head-dyke *n* a wall dividing the green pasture from the heather.

head-man *n* a stalk of rib-grass.

heathens *n* gneiss.

heather *n* heath.

heather-bill *n* a dragon-fly.

heather-birns *n* the stalks and roots of burnt heath.

heather-brae *n* a heather clad slope.

heather-cat *n* a cat becoming wild and roving among the heather.

heather-cow *n* a tuft or twig of heather; a sort of besom made of heath.

heathery-heidit *n* (used of a mountain) the summit clad with heather.

hech-howe *n* the name of the poisonous herb hemlock. This seems a fanciful designation for the expression of sorrow produced in consequence of any one having eaten of this noxious plant.

heel of the twilight *phr* the termination of twilight.

heeroad *n* highway.

heff, heft *n, v* dwelling; place of residence; to dwell; to accustom to live in a place.

heich *n* a slight elevation, as a pimple; a very small knoll.

heid-roume *n* the ground lying between a *haugh*, or flat, and the top of a hill.

heir downe *adv* below on this earth.

hellie-man's-rig *phr, n* a piece of land dedicated to the devil.

Hell's holes *n* those dark nooks that are dreaded as being haunted with bogles.

hen's cavey *n* a hen-house.

hen's croft *n* a portion of a

corn-field frequented and damaged by fowls.

hen's ware *n* the edible fucus.

henny-beik *n* honey hive.

herbere *n* a herb garden.

herbery *n* a military station; a haven or a harbour; a shelter; a small loch; a stream.

herd *n, v* one who tends cattle; to tend cattle, or to take care of a flock.

herdship, hereschip *v* the plundering of cattle.

herd-widdiefows *n* cattle-stealers.

herezeld *n* the best beast on the land, given to the landlord on the death of the tenant.

herison *n* hedgehog.

hersel, hirdsale, hirdsel *n* a flock of sheep etc.

het seed, hot seed *n* early grain.

hetherig, hiddrig *n* the ridge of land at the end of a field, on which the horses and plough turns.

heuch, heugh, hewch, huwe, hew *n* a crag; a ragged steep; a steep hill or bank; a glen with a steep overhanging *braes* or sides; a shaft, mine, coal-pit.

heuch-head *n* the top of a cliff or precipice.

hevin, hewin *n* a haven or harbour.

hewis *n* forms; ghosts.

hiddils, hidlings *n* hiding places.

high-gait *n* the high road; the public road.

hilch *n* a shelter from wind or rain.

hilch of a hill *phr* the brow or higher part of the face of a hill, whence one can get a full view, on both hands, of that side of the hill: it is distinguished from the *hip* of the hill, which is a sort of round eminence lower in situation than a *hilch*, and distinguished from the *ridge*, from which both the back and face of the hill may be seen.

hill-gait *n* a hilly road; a hill-road.

hill-head *n* the summit or top of a hill.

hillan *n* a hillock.

hilling *v* grazing on hill pasture.

hill-slack *n* a pass between two hills.

hill trow *n* spirits supposed to inhabit the hills of Orkney.

hill-worn *adj* wearied with hill-walking.

hin'-harvest-time, hin-hairst, hint o' hairst *n* that time of the year between harvest and winter, also the "back-end o' hairst".

hind-berries *n* raspberries.

hinny-bee *n* a working bee, as contrasted with a drone.

HOOICK

hip *n* the edge or border of any district of land; a round eminence situated towards the extremity, or on the lower part of a hill.

hirsell, hirseling *v* to class into different flocks; the act of separating into herds or flocks.

hirst *n* the bare and hard summit of a hill; a sandbank on the brink of a river; equivalent to *shallow* in a river; a resting-place; a small wood.

hive *n* a haven.

hiving-sough *n* the peculiar buzzing sound made by bees before they hive.

hoam *n* level, low ground beside a stream; a holm; an island in a lake; a depression; a hollow.

hobble-quo, -bog *n* a quagmire; soft, wet quaking ground.

hobblie *adj* (used of ground) soft, quaking underfoot.

hockerie-topner *n* the house-leek.

hoddle *n* a clumsy rick of corn.

hodlack *n* a rick of hay.

hodle *n* a small, roadside inn.

hogging *n* a place, whether enclosed or not, where sheep, after having arrived at the state of *hogs*, are pastured.

hoip *n* a hollow between hills.

holt *n* a wood; high and barren ground; a very small hay-cock, or a small quantity of manure before it is spread.

honey-ware *n* a species of edible seaweed.

hood-sheaf *n* the name given to each of the sheaves with which a stock or shock of corn is covered in the field, for carrying off the rain.

hooick, howick *n* a small stack in a field, built in a wet harvest.

hooloch, hurloch *n* a hurl of stones; an avalanche.

hoom *n* a herd, a flock.

hop, hope *n* a sloping hollow between two hills, or the hollow that is formed between two ridges on one hill; a haven; a small bay; a hill.

hop-clover *n* yellow clover.

hope-fit *n* the lowest part of a *hope* or valley among hills.

hope-head *n* the highest part of a *hope* or valley among hills.

horn-golach, hornie-gorlach *n* an earwig.

horse-knot *n* common black knapweed.

horse-stang *n* the dragon-fly.

horse-well-grass *n* common brook-lime, a herb.

hose-gerse, -grass *n* meadow soft grass.

howe o' the year *phr, n* the winter solstice.

houff, howff, howf *n* a place of resort or concourse; a haunt; a much frequented tavern; a shelter; a cemetery; a burial place.

howllis hald *n* a ruin; an owl's habitation.

huick *n* a small rick of corn.

humin *n* twilight.

humple *n* a hillock.

humplock *n* a small heap, such as of earth or stones, as in "the dirt is clautit into humplocks"; a little rising ground.

huntsman's moon *n* the October moon.

hurcham *adj* like a hedgehog.

hurcheon, hyrchoune *n* a hedgehog.

hurley house *n* a term applied to a large house, that is in so much disrepair as to be nearly in a ruinous state.

hurloch, urloch *n* a falling or rolling mass; an avalanche of sand, stones, etc.

husband-toon *n* a farmstead.

hut, hand-hut *n* a small stack built in the field; more generally it is used to denote a heap of any kind; a heap of dung laid out in the field.

hutch *n* a deep pool in a river underneath an overhanging bank; a small heap of dung; a small rick or temporary stack of corn; an embankment to hinder the water from washing away the soil.

hyrsale, hirsell, hirdsell, hirsle *n* a multitude; a throng; a flock of sheep.

I

imaky-amaky *n* an ant; a pismire.

in-country *n* the interior of a country; an inland district.

inbreak *n* a portion of the *infield* pasture-land broken up or tilled.

income-ware *n* weeds or wrack cast ashore by the sea.

infield *n* arable land continually cropped and matured.

ingaan-mouth *n* the mouth of a coal-pit with a horizontal direction.

ingers *n* grass or grass fields lying within the bounds of a town or village.

ingowne, ingane *n* a onion.

inks *n* low-lying lands on the banks of a river, overflowed by the sea at high-tide, and covered by short, coarse grass; shore pasture.

inscales *n* the racks at a lower end of a *cruive* in a river.

insh *n* low-lying land near a river.

inthrow and outthrow *adv, adj* in every direction.

iron-eer-well *n* a mineral well.

irr *n* a shepherd's call to a dog to pursue cattle.

J

jacky-forty-feet *n* a centipede.

Jacob's ladder *n* the belladonna.

jarness *n* a marshy place, or any place so wet as to resemble a marsh.

jaud *n* an old, done horse.

jenny-guid-spinner *n* the daddy-long-legs.

jenny-mony-feet *n* a species of centipede.

jicky *adj* (applied to a horse) startling.

jock-startle-a-stobie *n* the exhalations from the ground on a warm summer day.

johny-stan-still *n* a scarecrow.

K

kaim, kame *n* a low ridge; the crest of a hill; a camp or fortress; a mound.

kairney *n* a small heap of stones.

kairs *n* rocks through which there is an opening.

keavle *n* the part of a field which falls to one on a division by lots.

kemp *n* the name given to a stalk of ribgrass, *Plantago lanceolata.*

kemp *v* to fight, struggle, to compete, especially in the harvest field.

kemper *n* one who strives, now generally applied to reapers striving on the harvest-field.

kempin *v* the act of striving on the harvest field.

kemple *n* forty wisps or bottles of straw or hay.

kerse *n* an alluvial plain near a river.

ket *n* the weed called quack-grass; spongy peat, composed of tough fibres of moss and other plants; exhausted land.

ketty *adj* (used of grass) matted with couch grass; (used of peats) spongy, fibrous.

king-cup *n* the marsh marigold.

king-coll-awa', king-collie *phr, n* the lady-bird.

king's ellwand *n* the constellation properly called Orion's Girdle or Belt.

king's weather *n* the exhalations arising from the earth on a warm day.

kinnen, kippen *n* a rabbit.

kip *n* a sharp-pointed hill; those parts of a mountain which resemble round knobs, jutting out by the side of the cattle-path are called *kipps.*

kippie *n* a small hill.

kirkland *n* land belonging to the church.

kirk-brae *n* the hill on which a church stands.

kitty-langlegs *n* the daddy long-legs.

knab *n* the apex of a rock or hill; a rocky headland.

knibblockie *adj* (applied to a road) in which many small stones rise up; rough.

knock *n* a hill, a knoll; a little sheaf of cleaned straw of four or five inches in diameter.

knout-berry *n* the cloudberry.

know, knowe *n* a little hill.

krauperts *n* the crowberry.

kyle of hay *n* a hay-cock; the small heap into which hay is first gathered when it is raked from the ground.

L

lachterstead *n* the ground occupied by a house.

lady landers *n* the ladybird.

lade-sterne *n* the pole-star.

lady-bracken *n* the female fern.

lady-garten-berries *n* the bramble.

lady's (our) elwand *n* the vulgar designation of the constellation called Orion's Girdle.

lady's-fingers, ladies'-fingers *n* the kidney vetch.

lady's-smock, ladies'-smock *n* the cuckoo flower.

laich *n* a hollow, low-lying land.

laich country *n* the low country; the Lowlands.

laich croft *n* a low-lying croft.

laid *adj* (used of crops) flattened by a storm.

laing *n* a small ridge of land.

lair *n* a mire, a bog, quicksand; a patch of moss for drying peats.

lairach *n* the site of a building; the traces of a foundation or ruin; the foundation on which a stack rests; a peat moss; a cairn of stones.

lairie *adj* boggy, marshy.

lairoch *n* a site.

lambie, lammie *n* a small lamb.

lamb's-tongue *n* corn-mint.

Lammas *n* the beginning of August.

Lammas-nicht *n* the night of August the 1st.

Lammermoor lion *n* a sheep.

lammie sourocks *n* the herb sorrel.

lamp *v* the ground is said to *lamp*, when covered with cobwebs which appear after dew or slight frost.

land *n* a clear level place in a wood; the country.

land-stane *n* a stone found in the soil of a field.

landin' *n* the termination of a ridge; a term used by reapers in relation to the ridge on which they are working.

landtide *n* the undulating motion in the air, as perceived in a droughty day; the effect of evaporation.

lang *v* to belong; to become; to long.

lang halter time *n* the season of the year when, fields being cleared, travellers and others claimed a common right of occasional pasturage.

lang hame *n* the grave; heaven.

lang-leggit-tailor *n* the daddy long-legs.

laplove *n* climbing buckweed, *Corn convolvulus.*

lapron *n* a young rabbit.

larick *n* the larch.

larick's lint, laverock-lint, laverock's-lint *n* great golden maiden-hair; the dwarf-flax.

latch *n* a mire; a swamp.

law *n* a designation given to many hills or mounts, whether natural or artificial; a tomb, a grave, a mound; a roundish or conical hill.

lawland, lawlands *n* belonging to the low country of Scotland; the plain country of Scotland, as distinguished from the Highlands.

lawrie *n* a designation for the fox.

lay down *v* to sow out in grass.

laying time *n* the season when shepherds besmear their sheep with butter and tar to guard them against the cold of winter.

lea *adj* not ploughed; to remain some time without being cropped.

lea laik *n* a natural shelter for cattle such as is produced by glens or overhanging rocks.

lea-laik-gair *n* well sheltered grazing ground; sometimes applied to the place where two hills join together and form a kind of bosom.

leddy-launners *n* the ladybird.

leishin *adj* (as applied to a field, farm, parish etc.) extensive; (as referring to a journey) long.

leissure, lizzure *n* pasture between two corn fields; any grazing ground.

lepit-peats *n* peats dug out of the solid moss, without being baked.

lesuris *n* pastures.

licht-o'-day *n* the white phlox.

lie *n* the exposure; (applied to ground) a sheltered, warm place, as in "it has a warm lie".

lift *n* the firmament, the sky.

lift *v* to plough or break up ground; to ascend a brow, as in "to lift a brae".

lily-can *n* the yellow water-lily, *Nymphaea lutea.*

lime-craig *n* a lime quarry, a limestone cliff.

lime-quarrel *n* a lime quarry.

lime-work, -wark *n* a place where lime-stone is dug and burnt.

ling *n* a species of rush, or thin long grass.

links *n* the windings of a river, or the rich ground lying among these windings; the sandy flat ground on the sea-shore; sandy and barren ground though at a distance from any body of water.

linky *adj* flat and grassy.

lithe *n, adj* a shelter; sheltered.

lithesome *adj* sheltered; shady; warm; cosy.

lizzure *n* a pasture; grassland.

llarg *n, v* corn in a wet mass in the midst of a dry sheaf; to lodge in wet masses, as grass.

llauve-cairn *n* a beacon cairn.

loan *n* a lane; a narrow street; an opening between fields of corn, for driving the cattle homewards, or milking cows; a narrow enclosed way; a milking-park; a paddock; a small common.

loan-end *n* the end of a *loan.*

loan-head *n* the upper end of a

loan.

loaning *n* a lane; a bypath; a milking-park; a paddock.

loaning-dyke *n* a wall commonly of sods, dividing the arable land from the pasture.

loaning-green *n* a milking-green.

loch-reed *n* the common reed grass.

locken-gowlan, locker *n* the globe-flower.

lodge *v* (used of grain) to lie flat through wind or rain.

lonachies, lonnachs *n* couch-grass, *Triticum repens*; couch-grass gathered in heaps for burning.

lone *n* a place of shelter; a lane; an avenue; an entry to a place or village.

lonkor *n* a hole in a dyke through which sheep may pass.

lonyng, loning *n* a narrow enclosed way; the privilege of having a common through which cattle pass or return from pasture.

lopper-gowan *n* the yellow ranunculus which grows by the sides of streams.

lossie *adj* (applied to *braird*) the first shooting of grain, fields of grain, pulse etc. in which there are vacancies, as in "a lossie braird" or "the corn lan' is unco lossie this year".

lotch *n* a snare.

lover's loup *n* the leap of a despairing lover over a precipice; the place where such a leap has occurred.

lown-hill *n* the sheltered side of the hill.

lowrie, lowrie tod *n* the fox.

lubba *n* a coarse grass of any kind.

lucky-minnie's 'oo' *n* a fleecy substance growing on a plant in wet ground.

lye *n* pasture land.

lynyng *v* the act of measuring land, or of fixing the boundaries between contiguous possessions.

lyth *n* a shelter.

M

Macfarlane's bouat *n* the moon.

mae, may *n, v* the bleat of a sheep; to bleat softly.

maggie monyfeet, meggy-monyfeet, monyfeet *n* "Meg-wi-the-mony-feet", a centipede.

mahers *n* a tract of low land, of a marshy and moory nature.

maid-in-the-mist *n* navelwort, *Cotyledon umbilicus veneris.*

maiden *n* the last handful of corn cut down by the reapers on a farm; this being dressed up with ribbons, in resemblance of a young woman; the feast of harvest-home.

mail-garden *n* a garden, the products of which are raised for sale.

mailer, mealler *n* a cottager who gets some wasteland for a number of years, rent-free, to improve it.

mailie *n* a pet ewe.

mailin, mailing, maling *n* a farm, from *mail*, as being rented.

mails *n* a herb.

main-rig *adj* (applied to land) where the ridges are possessed alternately by different individuals.

mains *n* the farm attached to a mansion-house; the home-farm on an estate.

malkin *n* a hare; a half-grown girl.

mamore *n* a big field.

man-hive *n* a populous town.

manelet *n* corn marigold.

maoil *n* a promontory.

mappy *n* a rabbit.

mapsie *n* a pet sheep; a young hare.

march-balk *n* the narrow ridge which sometimes serves as the boundary between the land of different proprietors.

march-dike *n* a wall separating one farm or estate from another.

marche *v* to distinguish boundaries by placing landmarks.

marche, marchstane *n* a landmark.

margent *n* a margin; bank; beach.

marish *adj* marshy.

mark *adj* dark; mirky.

markland, mark-land *n* a division of land.

markstane *n* a landmark; a boundary-stone.

marsh-bent, marsh-bent-grass *n* the fine top grass.

martlet *n* a martin; more commonly *mertrick*, a kind of large weasel, which bears a rich fur.

mashlie-moss *n* a moss that is much broken up.

maukin *n* a hare.

may-spink *n* the primrose.

meadow *n* boggy land producing coarse grass.

meadow hay *n* the hay produced from bogs.

meadow-kerses *n* the cuckoo flower.

mealin, mealing *n* a farm; a holding; rent for a farm.

mealler *n* a cottager who, rent-free for many years, improves wasteland; a farmer paying rent.

meaner *n* an arbiter who adjusts in equal portions land held in common by various tenants.

mearen *n* a slip of uncultivated ground of various breadth, between two corn ridges; this seems the same with *mere*, a boundary.

meat-year *n* the season for crops etc.

meaths *n* maggots.

mede *n* a meadow.

medlert *n* this world.

meduart *n* meadow-sweet.

meed, meedge *n* a landmark.

meen *n* the moon.

meenlicht *n* moonlight.

meeran *n* a carrot.

meese, meethe, meeth *n, v* a measure; a mark; a landmark for vessels at sea; to mark a place at sea by the bearings of landmarks.

mekilwort *n* the deadly nightshade.

merch, mere, meth *n* a march; a boundary.

merry-dance, -dancers *n* the Aurora Borealis; the exhalations from the earth in a warm day, as seen flickering in the atmosphere.

merse *n* a fertile spot of ground between hills; alluvial land on the side of a river; ground gained from the sea, converted into moss.

metal *n, v* the stones used for making a road; to make or repair a road with broken stones.

mew *n* an enclosure.

mey *n, v* the bleat of lambs.

Michaelmas-moon *n* the harvest moon; the produce of a *raid* at this season, as constituting the portion of a daughter.

midden *n* a dunghill.

midden-monarch *n* a cock.

midden-scarter *n* a hen.

midden-tap *n* the top of a dung-hill; if a crow flies over a dunghill, it is viewed by some as a presage of bad weather.

middle-erd *n* the earth; the world; the nether regions.

midge *n* this not only denotes a gnat as in English but is used by the vulgar for a Scottish mosquito.

mids-day, midtime o' day *n* midday.

midwinter-day *n* the name anciently given to the brumal solstice.

mile *n* wild celery.

milk-gowan *n* a yellow flower whose stem contains a humour similar to buttlemilk; the dandelion, *Leontodon taraxacum.*

milkmaid's path *n* the milky way, or galaxy.

minister *n* small spiral shells found on the seashore.

mire *n* a bog, swamp.

mirk *v* to grow dark.

mirk monanday *n* a day of uncommon darkness, often referred to in the conversations of old people; (refers to) March 24th 1652, when the sun was totally eclipsed.

mirk-dim, mirky *adj* dark, gloomy, murky.

mirkin *n* darkness, nightfall.

mirran, mirrot *n* a carrot.

misgrow *v* to grow stunted, crooked, ill shaped.

misk *n* land covered with coarse, rough, moorish grasses.

misk-grass *n* the grass which grows on ground as described under *misk.*

mitherland *n* native land.

moch, moch-flea, mogh *n* a moth.

modywart, moldewort *n* a mole.

mold *n* the ground.

moleery-tea *n* the common milfoil; the goose tongue.

mone *n* the moon.

monteyle *n* a mount.

month, mounth *n* a mountain; the Grampian mountains towards their eastern extremity; to cross the Grampians, as in "to gang o'er the month".

monthis bord *n* (perhaps) the ridge or longitudinal summit of a mountain.

moo-maein *n, v* the lowing of cattle.

moodie, moodie-warp, moudie, mowdewarp, mowdiewart, mowdie, mowdy *n* a mole.

moodie-hill, moudie-hillan, mowdie-hillock, mowdie-hoop *n* a molehill.

mool *n* mould, soil good for working; pulverized dry earth; the soil for a grave; the grave.

moold *n* the ground, earth.

mooly *adj* mouldy, earthy, earth-stained; savouring of the grave.

moon-broch *n* a halo round the moon.

moor *n* peaty land; peat-mud.

moor-band *n* a surface of peat-moss wasted to a kind of light black earth, often mixed with sand.

moor-burn *n* the annual burning of part of a moor; an outbreak of temper; a dispute, conflict.

moor-hags *n* holes made in moor or moss by peat-cutting.

moory *adj* heathy; of a brown or heather colour.

moose *n* mouse.

mooseweb, mouse-web *n* gossamer; spider's web.

more, muir *n* a heath.

morning-blink *n* early morning light.

morning-mun *n* the dawn; increasing daylight.

moss *n* a marshy place; a place where peats may be cut.

mossfaw *n* a ruinous building.

moss-aik *n* bog oak, the trunks of ancient oak trees buried in a peat bog.

moss-boil *n* a fountain in the moss.

moss-corn *n* silver-weed.

moss-fa'en *adj* (applied to trees) overthrown in a morass and gradually covered with moss.

moss-fog *n* mosses growing in a bog or swamp.

moss-hag *n* a place out of which peats have been cut.

moss-leerie *n* a will-o'-the-wisp.

moss-thief *n* a Border reiver.

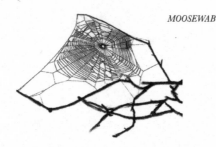

MOOSEWAB

moss-thistle *n* the marsh-thistle.

mossin'-time *n* the peat-cutting season.

mot, mote *n* a little hill, or barrow; sometimes improperly used for a high hill; a rising ground, a knoll.

moud *n* a moth.

moul, mould *n* the grave; soil.

mouldie *v* savouring of the grave.

mounth *n* a mountain.

mount-caper *n* the marsh orchid, *Orchis latifolia.*

mourie *n* a gravelly sea-beach; a stratum of gravel mingled with sand.

mourn *v, n* (used of cattle) to moan; a murmuring sound.

mowbeiraris *n* thievish gleaners.

mowe *n* dust.

moylie *n* a hornless bullock; a soft, good natured, silly person.

mugg-ewe *n* a sheep with a good coat of wool.

muggart, mugger *n* the mugwort.

muir *n* a heath.

muir-band, moor-band *n* a hard subsoil composed of clayey sand impervious to water.

mule, mull *n* a promontory.

munelichty *n* moonlight.

mure-burn *n, v* the burning of the heath.

mureland, moorland *n* pertaining of the moor; an upper and less cultivated region.

murelander, mureman *n* a dweller in a *mureland.*

muskane *adj* mossy.

mutton *n* a sheep.

myaakin *n* a hare.

mydill erd, medlert, midlert *n* this earth.

myis *n* mice.

nab *n* the summit of a rock or hill, a rocky headland.

naigie *n* a horse; a pony.

naitir *n* nature.

naitral *n, adj* native.

naked-corn *n* thin-eared corn.

nanny *n* a she-goat.

napple, napple root *n* the heath pea.

napsis *n* a little, fat animal, such as a sheep.

nashag *n* the bearberry.

nature *n* spontaneously producing rich herbage; land that produces rich grass without having been sown, as in "nature ground".

nature-clover *n* rich natural clover.

nature-grass *n* rich natural grass.

nature-ground *n* land producing rich natural grass.

nature-hay *n* hay produced by the ground spontaneously.

natureness *n* spontaneous fertility in rich herbage; richness and exuberance of natural grass.

naze *n* a promontory; a headland.

neap, neep *n* a turnip.

near-hand-gate *n* the nearest way.

near-hand-road *n* a short-cut.

neat land *n* land for grazing neat cattle.

neb-o'-the-morning *n* the time between dawn and sunrise.

neep-grun' *n* ground for growing turnips.

neep-reet *n* growing turnips.

nether, neddar, neddir *n* an adder.

nettercap, nettery *n* a spider.

neuk-time *n* the twilight; in reference to its being the season for pastime or gossiping among work-people.

nib *n* a narrow strip of land; a long, projecting headland.

night, nycht *v* to stop work for the day; to cease from labour when day-light closes.

nichting-time, nychtin-time *n* the time when out-door labour ceases during the winter season, i.e., when day-light closes.

nicht-hawk *n* a large white moth, which flies about hedges in summer evenings; a person who ranges about at night.

nicht-mirk *n* the darkness of night.

nicht, nicht-come *n, adv* night, the evening; nightfall.

nick *n* an opening between the summits of two hills.

nightingale *n* a moth.

nirb *n* anything of stunted growth.

nittle *n* nettle.

nob *n* a rounded hill.

nocks *n* little beautiful hills.

noit *n* a small rocky height.

nolt-tath *n* luxuriant grass.

norlins, north-bye *adj, adv, n* northward.

north-dancers *n* the Aurora Borealis.

nought, nout, nowt *n* cattle.

nut-brae *n* a *brae* abounding in hazel-nut trees.

O

overspade, owerspade, o'er-spade *v* to cut land into narrow trenches, heaping the earth upon an equal quantity of land not raised.

oachening *n, adv* early dawn; the night just before daybreak.

oak-eggar *n* a moth.

oe *n* a small island

offer *n* "offer of a brae", the projecting bank of a river that has been undermined by water.

offskep *n* the utmost boundary or limit in a landscape.

okragarth *n* a stubble-field.

old man's fold *n* a portion of ground devoted to the devil.

onker *n* a small portion of land.

onland *n* a designation of land, occurring in ancient charters.

onpricket *adj* (used of cattle) without pricking or startling in hot weather.

ontron *n, adv* evening.

orchin *n* a hedgehog.

ord *n* a steep hill or mountain; a point of land, a promontory or headland.

oubit *n* a butterfly in the caterpillar

state; a hairy caterpillar.

ouer-by, overby *adj, adv* a little way across.

ouerway *adj, adv, n* the upper or higher way.

ourach *n* a potato.

out-dyke, out-o'-dykes *adj* in unfenced pasture.

outen *adj, prep, adv* out of doors.

outbreck, outbrek *n* a portion of *outfield* or pasture-land newly broken up or prepared for cultivation.

outca' *n* a pasture to which cattle are *caw'd* or driven out.

outrun *n* pasture land attached to a farm.

outshot *n* pasture; untilled ground.

outside worker *n* a field worker.

outsucken *n* the freedom of a tenant from bondage to a mill.

outland *adj* outlying; lying on the borders of a burgh.

outlander *n* an alien, a stranger; an incomer to a burgh or parish; also one who lives beyond the bounds of a burgh.

owrdrevin *adj* (applied to land covered by the drifting of sand) overrun.

owrter *adj, adv* further over.

oxgate, oxengate, oxgang *n* a measure of land varying according to the nature of the soil.

P

paal *n* a post; a mooring post.

packman-rich *n* a species of bear or barley having six rows of grains on the ear.

packs *n* the sheep, male or female, that a shepherd is allowed to feed along with his master's flock, this being in lieu of wages.

padda, paddan *n* a frog.

paddie-stule, paddock stool,

peddock-stule *n* a toadstool; a term of contempt.

paddock-pipes *n* marsh horse-tail.

paddokstane *n* the toadstone, vulgarly supposed to grow in the head of a toad; accounted precious on account of the virtues ascribed to it – both medical and magical.

paffle *n* a small possession of land.

paid *n* a path; a steep ascent.

paidle *v* to hoe.

pailin *n* a fence made of stakes.

paip *n* thistle down.

paithment *n* the pastures.

paley-lamb *n* a very small or feeble lamb.

pamphil *n* a square enclosure made with stakes; any small house.

pan *n* a hard impenetrable crust below the soil.

pare *v* to cut off the surface of a moss or moor; to run a plough lightly among thinned turnips to check weeds.

park-dyke *n* a field-dyke, or wall of stone or turf enclosing a field.

parochrie *n* parish.

parrach, parrich, parrick *n* a small field, a paddock; a small enclosure in which a ewe is confined to suckle a strange lamb; a crowd; a collection of things huddled together; a group.

part *n* a place, a district.

particate *n* a rood of land.

particle *n* a small piece of land.

partiere-wall *n* a boundary wall common to two proprietors.

path *n* a steep and narrow way; the world; the way through life.

pathlins *adj, adv* by a steep and narrow way.

pays *n* a road leading from the town to the country.

pease-bogle *n* a scarecrow set up in a field of peas.

peasy-whin *n* the greenstone.

peat claig *n* a place built to hold peats.

peat-breest *n* the peat bank.

peek *n* the sharp point of a sea-cliff or rock.

peekie *n* a small ray or point of light.

peelie *n* a scarecrow.

peirs *adj* sky-coloured.

pen *n* a conical top, generally in a range of hills.

pen-fauld *n* the close or yard near a farmer's house for holding his cattle.

pendicle *n* a small piece of ground.

penhead *n* the upper part of a *mill-lead*, where the water is carried off from the dam to the mill.

pete-pot *n* a hole from which peats have been dug.

Peter's Pleugh *n* the constellation Ursa Major, so named in honour of Peter the Apostle.

Peter's Staff *n* Orion's Sword, or Belt, a constellation. *See also* Lady's

Elwand.

peth *n* a steep and narrow way.

pheer *v* in ploughing, to mark off the ridges by one or two furrows.

pheerin *v, n* the act of turning a plough; the furrow or furrows that mark off the breadth of the ridges.

pict's houses *n* the name given to those mounds which contained cellular enclosures under ground.

piege *n* a trap, a snare.

pik-mirk *adj* dark as pitch.

pikes *n* short withered heath.

pinkie *n* the clove-pink.

pirl-grass *n* creeping wheat-grass.

pishminnie *n* an ant.

piss-the-bed *n* dandelion.

pit *n* a conical heap of potatoes partially sunk in a pit and covered with earth.

pit-bank *n* the bank around a pit.

pit-mirkness *n* intense darkness.

pit-stones *n* boundary-stones that mark different parts of a peat-moss.

plackit *n* (perhaps) trodden down.

plainstanes *n* the pavement.

plant-cot *n* a small enclosure for rearing cabbage-plants.

planting *n* a plantation.

plantry *n* garden grounds, plantations.

plant-toft *n* a bed for rearing young cabbage.

plenish *v* to stock a farm.

pleuch *n* a plough; the constellation called Ursa Major, supposed to resemble a plough.

pleuch-gang, pleuch-gate, plough-gate *n* as much land as can be properly tilled by one plough; a *plough-gate* or *plough-gang* is now understood to include about forty Scots acres at an average.

pleuch-land *n* arable land.

plies *n* thin strata of freestone.

plit *n* the slice of earth turned over by the plough.

pluff *n* a species of fungus called "the devil's snuff-mill", which, when rotten and dried, goes to dust as soon as touched.

plumrock *n* the primrose.

poffle *n* a small farm; a piece of land.

poldach *n* marshy ground lying on the side of a body of water; a marsh, a meadow on the shore.

policy *n* the pleasure-ground about a gentleman's seat.

pone *n* a thin turf.

pone *v* to pare off the surface of land.

pones *n* long meadow-grass.

poor man's weather-glass *phr, n*
the common pimpernel; the
knotted figwort.

poppill *n* corn campion or cockle.

post *n* stratum in a quarry.

pot *n* a pit; a dungeon, a pond
or pit full of water; a pool or
deep place in a river; a deep hole
scooped out in a rock by the eddies
in a river; a moss-hole from whence
peats have been dug; a shaft or pit
in a mine.

potato-bogle, -doolie *n* a
scarecrow.

potato-mould *n* a field on which
potatoes have been grown, and
which is considered rich enough to
give a crop of oats without further
manure.

pouder *n* dust.

pounce *n* long meadow-grasses.

poverty-pink *n* the clover *Trifolium*

poyndfalt *n* a fold in which cattle
were confined as being *poinded* or
distrained.

pray *n* a meadow.

pretty-dancers *n* the Aurora
Borealis.

priest's pintle *n* the rose-root.

prodler *n* a small horse, which
takes short steps.

proochie *n* a call to a cow to draw
near.

prop *v* to designate by landmarks.

ptru, ptroo, pru *v* to call to a
horse or cow to stop or approach.

puddock-stool *n* a mushroom, a
toad-stool.

pulaile *n* poultry.

pulder *n* powder, dust.

pull ling *n* a moss plant.

punckin, punkin *n* the footsteps
of horses or cattle to soft ground.

pund *n* a smaller fold for sheep.

pundler, punler *n* one who
watches fields or woods to prevent
thefts and impound straying cattle.

pushlock, puslick *n* cows' dung
dropped in the fields; dung of
cattle, horses, and sheep.

pyat-horse *n* a piebald horse.

Q

qua, quaa, quag, quhawe *n* a bog, a marsh a quagmire.

quaking-bog *n* a moving quagmire.

quaking, quakkin *adj* (used of a bog) moving, trembling.

quarrel *n* a stone quarry.

quaw *n* a quagmire; "bobbin's quaw", a spring or *wallee*, over which a tough sward has grown, sufficient to support a person's weight.

Queen Anne's thrissel *n* the musk-thistle.

quey, quy, quyach, quoyach, quroch, quyok, quaig *n* a cow of two years old; a heifer.

queyl *n* a haycock.

quhaip, quhawp *n* an evil spirit; a goblin supposed to haunt the eaves of houses at night on the lookout for evil-doers.

quhit, quhytt *n* wheat.

quhitred, quhittret *n* the weasel.

quhyn, quhin-stane *n* green-stone; the name given to basalt, trap etc.

quicken *n* couch grass.

quinter *n* a ewe in her third year.

quoy *n* a young cow.

quoyland *n* land taken in from a common, and enclosed.

quyle *n* a cock of hay.

R

ra, rae *n* a roe deer.

raab *n* a mass of rock, fallen, from a cliff.

rabbie-rinnie-hedge *n* the goose-grass.

rack *n* couch-grass, *Triticum repens*.

rae *n* an enclosure for cattle.

raffy *adj* (used of corn) rank, coarse, rapidly growing; (used of a crop) thick and thriving.

rag-fallow *n* a species of fallow.

rag-fauch, -faugh *n* land broken up in the summer after the hay is cut and ploughed three times and then dunged.

ragweed *n* ragwort.

rairuck *n* a small rick of corn.

raith *n* the fourth part of a year.

ramle *n* rubbish; fragments of stones, a wall etc. unsubstantially built; a heap of ruins; brushwood.

ramps *n* a species of garlic; wild garlic.

rangel *n* (applied to stones) a heap.

rannoch *n* bracken.

ranty-tanty *n* a weed which grows among corn, with a reddish leaf.

rapple *v* to grow quickly and in a rank manner; originally applied to quick vegetation.

rashy *adj* covered with rushes.

raskill *n* a young deer.

ratchel *n* a hard rocky crust below the soil.

ratchell *n* the stone called *wacken-porphyry.*

rathy *n* a good, quick-growing crop of hay, weeds.

ratton *n* a rat.

rauns *n* the beard of barley.

raw *v, n* (used of corn) to grow soft; undiluted whisky.

ray *n* rye.

razer *n* a measure of grain.

razon-berry *n* the red currant.

reath, reth, rett *n* the quarter of the year.

RANNOCH

63

rebleat *v* (used of a ewe) to bleat in response to her lamb.

red land *n* ground turned up by the plough.

red-doup *n* a kind of bumble bee.

red-neb *n* the vulgar name for the kidney bean potato.

redeven *n* "the evening of Beltane", (perhaps) rather the eve of Beltane, or the evening preceding that day.

ree *n* a permanent sheepfold surrounded with a wall of stone and *feal*, as in "a sheep-ree".

ree ruck *n* a small rick of corn put up to be easily dried.

reed *n* a cattle-yard; a bay; a roadstead.

reefort *n* a radish.

reegh, reigh *n* a harbour.

reeling *v* a whirling motion made by bees.

reesk *n* coarse grass that grows on downs; waste land, yielding only benty grasses; a marshy place.

reeskie *adj* abounding in *reesk*; coarse grass.

reeslin'-dry *adj* so dry as to make a rustling sound as corn when ripe.

reet *v* to turn up the ground with the snout.

reeve *n* a pen for cattle.

reezlie *adj* (applied to ground that has a cold bottom) producing coarse grass; coarse grass that grows on downs.

reid day *n* a day in September, before which wheat is generally sown. On *reid-een*, or the eve of this day, the hart and hind are believed to meet for copulation.

reid-een *n* the evening preceding the third day of May.

reisk, reisque *n* coarse grass growing on downs; a morass.

reive *n* a name given to what is considered to be an ancient Caledonian fort.

rendal, rennal, rennet, rundale *n* a division of land equivalent to a *run-rig*.

rennet *n* land held by tenants in places here and there, or land held by several tenants in one field, as in "rig and rennet".

resp *n* long coarse grass; a stalk of straw; a bulrush.

reuk *n* atmosphere.

reuth *n* wild mustard-seed.

reyss *n* coarse grass in marshy ground.

rhind *n* a footpath, a roadway.

rhone *n* a small patch of ice formed on a road.

rib land *v* to give it a half ploughing.

ribe, rybe *n* a colewort that grows tall with little or no leaf.

rickle *v* to put into a heap, as in "when are ye gaun to rickle your peats?".

rickly *adj* like stones loosely built; dilapidated, as in "rickly wa's".

ride *v* to ford on horseback; to be fordable on horseback; to ride on a plundering raid.

riding-time *n* the breeding season of sheep.

rig, rigg *n* a ridge; a long narrow hill; the spine of a person or animal; the space between the furrows of a field; a section of a ploughed field.

rig and bauk *n* a field with alternate strips of corn and pasture.

rig and fur *n* the ridge and furrow of a ploughed field; the whole field.

rig-and-rendal *n* the old land system of *runrig* where the small farms are parcelled out in discontiguous plots.

rig-head *n* the strip of land at the sides of a field where the plough turns.

rimpin *n* a lean cow.

rinse-heather, ringe-heather, rinze-heather *n* the cross-leaved heather.

rinker *n* a tall, thin, long-legged horse.

ripplin-garss *n* rib-grass.

rise *n* a coarse kind of grass.

risk *n* wet, boggy land.

riskish *adj* (applied to soil) land of a wet and boggy nature, as in "riskish lan".

risp, rispie *n* coarse grass that grows on marshy ground.

rit-fure *n* the first furrow opened in ploughing; a furrow to run off surface water in a ploughed field.

rive *v* to plough, spoken of ground that is very tough or has been long unploughed; (used of clouds) to break; (used of a storm) to rage.

rizzim *n* a stalk of corn.

rizzle *v* to rustle; anything such as straw, is said to be *rizzling*, when it is free of moisture, quite dry; to rustle.

rizzle-buss *n* a red-currant bush.

road-money *n* a tax for the maintenance of the public roads.

road-reddens *n* mud raked to the side in cleaning roads.

road-stoor *n* dust on the road.

roar *v* to emit a loud continuous report, as the cracking of a field of ice.

robin-rin-the-hedge *n* the goosegrass; a trailing kind of weed which runs along hedges.

roche *adj, n* (applied to sheep) unshorn; a rock.

A *Scots* Dictionary *of Nature*

rocking-stane *n* a great stone so poised by art as to move at the slightest touch.

rockle *n* a pebble.

rocklie *adj* abounding with pebbles.

roddie *n* a narrow road; a short footpath.

roddin *n, v* a sheep-track; making tracks or narrow paths.

roist *n* a roost.

ronnachs *n* couch-grass.

roo *n* an enclosure in a grass field, in which cattle are penned up during the night.

roof-rotten *n* the black rat.

roplaw *n* a young fox.

roseir *n* a rose-bush, or arbour of rose.

rosen, rossen *n* a congeries or cluster of shrubs or bushes.

rosin *n* a bramble-thicket.

rot-grass *n* the midge-grass.

rottacks *n* grubs in a bee-hive.

rotton, rotten *n* the rat.

rouch girs *n* rough, benty grass; the rough cocksfoot-grass.

round-sound *n* the seed vessels of the honesty.

royal bracken *n* the flowering of the royal fern.

ruddin *n, adj* the berry of the mountain ash; anything very sour.

rudge *v* to gather stones into small heaps.

ruech, ruith *n* a hill pasture, cattle run; summer run; summer sheiling.

rumgunshoch *adj* (applied to soil) rocky, stony.

rummlekirn *n* a gully on rocky ground; a gully on a wild, rocky shore.

runches *n* the largest kind of wild mustard.

runnie *n* a hog.

runrig *n* lands are said to lie *runrig* where the alternate ridges of a field belong to different proprietors, or are occupied by different tenants.

ruralach *n* a native of the rural world.

russa *n* a stallion.

ryfe *v* to plough up land that has been lying in waste, or in pasturage.

rype *v* to reap.

S

saan *n* sand.

sadjell *n* a lazy unwieldy animal.

Saint Peter's wort *n* the *Hypericum* or hard-hay.

sair-six *n* a rotation of crops, two of each of grass and cereals, one of turnips, and one of cereals.

salebrosity *n* a rough place.

sanape *n* mustard.

sand-bunker *n* a small well fenced sand-pit.

Sandy Campbell *n* a pig.

sanglere *n* a wild boar.

sat *n* a snare.

saving-tree *n* the sabine, a plant. "Saving-tree is said to kill the foetus in the womb. It takes its name from this, as being able to save a young woman from shame. This is what makes gardeners and others wary about giving it to females."

scabbit *adj* (used of land) thin, bare, gravelly, rocky; (used of vegetation) thin, patchy, mean, paltry.

scad, scade *n* any colour seen by reflection; or the reflection itself.

scaddaw *n* a shadow.

scaldricks *n* wild mustard.

scallion *n* a leek.

scalp *n* land of which the soil is very thin.

scannachin *adj* glancing, as light.

scape *n* a bee-hive.

scar *adj, n* wild, not tamed; a bare place on the side of a steep hill, from which the sward has been washed down by the rains; a cliff precipice; a spit of sand running into a lake or loch.

scarrow *n* faint light.

scaud, scawd *n* the appearance of light; a faint gleam.

scaud o' day *phr, n* the daybreak.

scaum o' the sky *phr, n* the thin vapour of the atmosphere.

scaup *n* a small bare knoll.

scaur *n* a bare place on the side of a hill; a cliff.

scaw *n* an isthmus or promontory.

schaddow half *n* that portion of land which lies towards the north, or is not exposed to the sun.

schald *n* a shallow place.

schawe *v* to sow.

schell-paddock *n* the land-tortoise.

schluchten *n* a hollow between hills.

schor *adj* steep; abrupt.

schugh *n* a furrow, a trench.

schyr *n* a shire; a division of land less than a county, sometimes only a parish.

sclate, sclaite *n* slate.

sclate-band *n* a stratum of slate among bands of rock.

sclater *n* a wood-louse.

sclater's eggs *n* little white eggs like beads, found in ploughed land.

scleeberie, sclibbrie, sclib-berie *n* a large piece of land of little value.

sclender, sclenter *n* loose thin stone lying on the face of a *scaur*; the face of a hill covered with small, loose stones.

sclenderie *n* covered with small loose stones.

sclent, sklent, sklin *v* to give a slanting direction.

sclithers *n* loose stones lying in great quantities on the side of a rock or hill.

scluchten *n* a flat-lying ridge.

sclutt *n* soft and coarse till.

scob-seibow *n* an onion that is allowed to remain in the ground during winter; the young shoot from an onion of the second year's growth.

scog *v* to shelter; to secrete.

scoggy, scokky *adj* shady; full of shades.

score *n* a deep, narrow, ragged indentation on the side of a hill.

scotch *n* an ant or emmet.

scotch-gale *n* the bog myrtle.

scraigh-o' day, scraik-o' day, screigh-o' day *phr, n* the first appearance of dawn.

screel *n* a large rocky hill nigh the sea; a haunt for the fox.

screw *n* a small stack of hay.

scrooby-grass, scrubie-grass *n* scurvy-grass.

scruffin *n* a thin covering or scurf; the surface of earth.

scruffin-time *n* the time for preparing land for one crop in succession to another, and covering the seed.

scuff *v* to graze; to touch lightly.

scug *n, v* a shade; a sheltered place; the declivity of a hill; to shade; to shelter, protect; to hide; to take shelter, refuge.

scurdy *n* a moor stone; a resting place; a favourite seat.

scurrie *adj, n* dwarfish; low

dwarfish thorns in muirland glens.

seater *n* a meadow.

seed-fur *n* the furrow into which the seed is to be cast.

seg, segg *n* the yellow flower-de-luce, *Iris pseudacorus.*

segg-backit *adj* applied to a horse whose back is hollow or fallen down.

seggy *adj* abounding with sedges.

seibow *n* a young onion.

seitis *n* plants or herbs.

set, sett *n* a potato, or part of one used for planting.

setnin *n* a motherless lamb, brought up by the hand.

sets *n* corn in small stacks.

settrels *n* the name given to the sprouts that shoot forth in spring from the coleworts planted in the beginning of winter.

seuch, seugh, sough *n* a furrow; a ditch; a drain.

seuin sternes *n* the Pleiades.

shade *n* a cultivated field.

shadow-half *n* the northern exposure of the land, the shady side.

shag *v* the refuse of barley; the term is sometimes applied to the refuse of oats.

shairn *n* the dung of cattle.

shak-and-tremble *n* the quaking grass.

shallochy *adj, n* shallow; land of a shallow nature, as in "shallochy land".

shalt *n* a horse of the smallest size.

shamloch *n* a cow that has not calved for two years.

shank *v* to sink a coal-pit, as in "to shank for coals".

shank of a hill *n* the projecting point.

shannach *n* a bonfire lighted on Hallow-eve.

shannel *n* subsoil; hard, unyielding subsoil as the foundation of a building.

shap *n* the soil at the foot of a wall, hedge, etc.

shargar *n, v* an ill-thriven person or animal; to stunt in growth; to become stunted.

shargar-stone *n* a stone which was supposed to stop the growth of any one who crept underneath it.

shargie *adj* thin; shrivelled.

sharn, shearn, shairn *n* the dung of oxen or cows.

shaul, shawl *adj* shallow; used in the proverb "shawl water maks mickle din".

shaw *n* a piece of ground which becomes suddenly flat at the bottom of a hill or steep bank, thus *birken-shaw*, a piece of ground, of the description given, covered with short scraggy birches; *brecken-shaw*, a shaw covered with ferns.

sheal, schele, sheil, sheald, shield, shieling, sheelin *n* a hut for those who have the care of sheep or cattle; a hut for fishermen; a shed for sheltering sheep during night; a nest for a field mouse.

sheal, shiel *v* to put sheep under cover.

shear *v* to cut down corn with the sickle; to reap in general.

shear of a hill *n* the ridge or summit, where wind and water are said to *shear*.

shearer *n* one employed in cutting down corn; in general sense, a reaper.

shearin *v* the act of cutting down corn.

shed *n* a portion of land, as distinguished from that which is adjacent; "a shed of corn", a piece of ground on which corn grows, as distinguished from the adjacent land on either side; "sick man's shed", a battle-field.

sheddin' *v* the act of separating the lambs from the parent ewes.

sheeling-hill *n* the eminence near a mill where the kernels of grain were separated, by the wind, from the husks.

sheep-bucht, -bught *n* small sheep-fold.

sheep-faws *n* retreats beneath the moors for sheep in winter.

sheep-gang *n* pasturage for sheep.

sheep-lifting *v* sheep stealing.

sheep-rodding *n* a sheep track.

sheep-rot *n* butterwort, a herb.

sheep-siller *n* common mica.

sheep-stell *n* an enclosure for sheep.

sheep-smearing *v* an application of tar and melted butter to sheep in winter for warmth.

sheep-taid *n* a tick or sheep-louse.

sheep-tathing *v* the confinement of sheep to a particular portion of ground until their droppings manure it.

sheep-tothins, -troddles *n* the droppings of sheep.

sheep's-cheese, -sowruck *n* the root of dog-grass, *Triticum repens.*

sheermouse *n* the shrew, or fieldmouse.

sheil, shield *n* a hut for shepherds.

sheiling *n* a temporary residence for shepherds etc.

sheiling-hill, shilling-hill *n* a winnowing-hill.

shellaggy *n* the *Tussilago,* or colt's-foot.

shelter-stell *n* an enclosure or shelter for sheep, of stone or a clump of trees.

sheltie *n* a horse of the smallest size.

shepherd-land *n* pastoral districts.

shepherd's needle *n* the wild chervil.

sheroo *n* the shrew-mouse.

sheuch *v* to lay plants in the earth, before they are planted out.

shiacks *n* light black oats, variegated with gray stripes, having beards like barley.

shift *n* a rotation of crops.

shillacks, shillocks, sheelocks *n* the lighter part of oats; the light grain that is blown aside in winnowing.

shin of a hill *n* the prominent or ridgy part of the declivity, with a hollow on each side.

shinicle *n* a bonfire lighted on Halloween.

shiolag *n* wild mustard.

shirrow *n* a species of fieldmouse.

shirt *n* the winter rape; wild mustard.

shoad *n* a portion of land.

shog-bog, shugbog *n* a deep mossy puddle, often that through which a spring takes its course, covered with a coating of closely matted grass, sufficiently strong to carry a light person, who, by giving a *shog*, produces an undulating motion.

sholt *n* a small horse.

shood *n* the distant noise of animals passing.

short sheep *n* a blackfaced forest breed of sheep.

shot *n* a half-grown swine; "a shot of ground", a plot of land.

shot brae *n* an avalanche causing a *scar* on a hillside or bank.

shot-heuch *n* an acclivity, especially on the brink of a river, of which the sward or surface has fallen down, in consequence of being undermined by the stream, or loosened by the water from above.

shot-star *n* that meteoric substance often seen to shoot through the atmosphere, or appearing in a gelatinous form on the ground.

shott *n* an ill-grown ewe.

shoulder *n* the slope of a hill.

shriek o' day, skreigh o' day *phr* daybreak.

shuckenwort *n* chickweed.

shurg *n* wet, gravelly subsoil.

shurlin *n* a sheep newly shorn.

shuttle o' ice *phr* a miniature glacier; a sloping side on which children can toboggan.

sickie *n* a sheep call.

sickly-looking *adj* (used of the moon) hazy, watery.

sillar shakle *n* the name of a plant.

siller-gringlers *n* the quaking-grass

siller-hair-grass *n* the mouse-grass.

simmer-lift *n* the summer sky.

sink *n* ground where there is a superabundant moisture; the pit of a mine.

sinwart *prep* towards the sun.

sitfast *n* creeping crowfoot, *Ranunculus repens*; a large stone fast in the earth.

sitteringis *n* (perhaps) denoting stones of a citron, or pale yellow colour.

sittie-fittie *n* the lady-bird.

sivven *n* the raspberry.

skair *n* a bare place on the side of a hill.

skairs *n* rocks through which there is an opening.

skathie *n* a fence.

skeebrie *n* thin, light soil.

skeo, skio *n* a hut for drying fish.

skeoch *n* a very small cave; a large chink in a cliff.

skep *n, v* a bee-hive made of twisted straw; "to skep a bike", to carry off wild bees, with their combs, from their natural nest, and put them in a hive, a practice common among boys.

sker, skerr *n* a ridge or rock; a bare precipice.

skerdins *n* mice.

skerry *n* an insulated rock; a flat rock, over which the sea flows when the tide rises.

skick, skich *v* (used of cattle) to frisk about.

skift *n* a broad ridge of land, as distinguished from *laing*, a narrow ridge. *See also* shed.

skillocks *n* wild mustard.

skimmer *n, v* the flickering of the rays of light; (applied to light) to flicker; used to denote the inconstant motion of the rays of light, when reflected from a liquid surface slightly agitated.

skir *n* a rock in the sea; a small rocky islet; a cluster of rocks.

skirlag *n* a long thin leaf, as of corn, held stretched between the thumbs held parallel, which, when blown upon, emits a musical sound.

skirvin' *n* a thin coating of snow, earth, etc.

sklidder *n* a place on the side of a hill where a number of small stones are collected.

skookin *n* sheep

skrew *n* a stack of corn or hay.

skruddack *n* a crevice in a rock.

skug *n* a shade; what defends from the heat; a shelter from storm; a shadow, or what causes partial obscurity; metaphorically applied to ghosts, in relation to the place of their residence.

skug *v* to shelter; to screen; to seek shelter from something, as in "to skug a shower"; to flee for shelter.

skuggy *adj* shady.

skule *n* a great collection of animals.

skurrie *n* a cow with *skurs*, or small horns.

sky *n* "the sky of a hill", the ridge or summit, whence water runs equally to one side or another; the light at the eastern horizon before sun-rise, or at the western after sunset; thus, "was ye up afore the sin the day?" "ay, afore the sky", or "the sky winna set this hour yet"; "between the sun and the sky", a phrase used to denote the interval between daybreak and sunrise.

skybrie *n* thin, light soil.

skyme *v* to glance or gleam with reflected light. It differs from *skimmer*, which seems to have a common origin, as *skimmer* is often applied to the luminous object itself.

skytes *n* hemlock.

slack *n* an opening between hills; a hollow; a pass; a glade; a hollow, boggy place.

slade *n* a hollow between rising grounds, one with a streamlet flowing in it.

slaid *n* a valley between two hills.

slait *n* the track of cattle among standing corn.

slak, slack, slake *n* an opening in the higher part of a hill or mountain, where it becomes less steep and forms a sort of pass; a gap or narrow pass between two hills or mountains; a morass.

slammachs *n* the gossamer.

slap *n* a narrow pass between two hills.

slay *v* to pulverize soil too much by harrowing.

slayworm *n* the slow-worm or blind-worm.

sleek, sliek *n* a measure of fruit, etc. containing 40lb.

sleetch *n* a kind of fat mud, taken from shores to manure land.

slob-lands *n* flat, muddy foreshores.

slock *n* a hollow between hills.

sloggy *adj* slimy; marshy.

slonk *n* a mire; a ditch.

sloom *v* (applied to flowers and plants touched by the frost) to become flaccid.

slot *n* a hollow in a hill, or between two ridges, as in "slot of a hill".

slouch *n* a deep ravine or gully.

sluchten *n* a flat-lying ridge.

slug, slug-road *n* a road through a narrow defile between two hills.

slump *n* a marsh, a swamp.

slump *v* to sink in a mire; to go down as a person through ice, or in a bog; to stick in a mire.

slumpie *adj* marshy, swampy.

slunk *n* a slough, a quagmire.

slusch *n* plashy ground.

slute *n* a slow, lazy animal, either man or beast.

sluther *n* a quagmire.

slype *v* to fall over, as a wet furrow from the plough.

smair-docken, smear-dokee, smear docken *n* the common dock; the good King Henry; both of which were used in making a salve for stings, sores etc.

smearing-house *n* the hut in which sheep are smeared.

smook *v* to suffocate by burning sulphur; a term applied to the mode of destroying bees in order to gain their honey.

snab *n* the projecting part of a rock or hill; the bank, rock, or hill itself,

which projects.

snappering-stone *n* a stumbling stone.

snaw-breakers *n* sheep scraping the hardened surface of the snow to find food.

sneck-pin *v* to put in small stones between the larger ones in a wall, and daub the seams with lime.

sned-kail *n* colewort or cabbages of which the old stalks, after they have begun to sprout, are divided by a knife and set in the earth for future product.

sneer *n, v* the hiss of an adder.

snuk, snuke *n* a small promontory.

speedart *n* the spider.

spout *n* a boggy spring in ground.

sockin-hour *n, adv* the portion of time between day-light and candle light.

soddle, sod-seat *n* a seat made of sod.

sodger's buttons *n* the white burnet-rose.

sodger's feather *n* the plant honesty.

son-afore-the-father *n* the common coltsfoot, *Tussilago farfara*.

sone pleucht *n* a ploughgate or division of land exposed to solar rays.

sonie half *n* that part of lands

which lies to the south or is exposed to the sun. This is opposed to the *schaddow half.*

sookie, sookie-soo *n* the flower of the red clover.

sookie-soorach *n* the common wood-sorrel, and other acid plants.

sooleen *n* the sun.

soor-leek, soorlick, soorick, soorock, sourlock, sourock, sourack *n* the common sorrel.

soor-grass *n* sedge grass.

sooth-side *n* the bright, sunny side.

soothlin' *adj, adv, n* southerly.

sootipillies *n* a moss plant which grows on a thick stock like a willow-wand. The head is about half a foot long, and of a *sootie* colour.

sootipirlies *n* bullrushes.

sotter *n* an indefinite number of insects or small animals collected together.

soum *n* the relative proportion of cattle or sheep to pasture, or vice versa; "a soum of sheep", five sheep, in some places ten; "a soum of grass", as much as will pasture one cow, or five sheep.

soum land *v* to calculate and fix what number of cattle or sheep it can support.

soum and roum *v* to pasture in summer and fodder in winter.

sour-grass *n* sedge-grass, a species of carex.

sour-land *n* land which, when left untilled, either becomes swardless from too much moisture, or produces nothing but sedge-grasses and other worthless aquatic plants.

sow-brock, soo-brock *n* a badger.

sow-crae *n* a pigsty.

sow-kill *n* a lime kiln dug out of the earth.

sowm *n* the number of sheep or cattle proportioned to a pasture; as much grass as will pasture one cow or five sheep.

sownack *n* a Hallowe'en bonfire.

spaining-time *n* the season for weaning lambs.

spangie *n* an animal fond of leaping.

sparty *adj* abounding in rushes.

speedard, speedart *n* a spider.

speengie-rose *n* the peony.

spin-Maggie, -Mary *n* a daddy long-legs.

spinning-jenny *n* the long-legged fly.

spire *v* to wither, denoting the effect of wind or heat.

spitty, spittie *n* the horse.

spoach, spoatch *v* to poach.

spotty *n* a designation of a fox.

spout *n* a boggy spring in ground.

spoutiness *n* the state of having many boggy springs.

spouty *adj* marshy; springy.

sprat, spratt, spret, sprett *n* the jointed-leaved rush; long, rough grass growing on marshy places.

spretty, sprithy *adj* full of rushes.

sprot *n* the withered stump of any plant, broken and lying on the ground; the end of grain, or branch blown from a growing tree, in consequence of high winds.

spunkie *n* a will-o'-the-wisp.

spunkie-haunted *adj* haunted by will-o'-the-wisps.

spunkie-howe *n* a hollow haunted by will-o'-the-wisps.

spy-knowe *n* a hill on which a watch is set.

squach, squagh *n, v* the noise a hare makes when a-killing.

squair *n* a gentle depression between two hills.

stable *n* that part of a marsh, in which, if a horse is foundered is said to be *stabled* for the night.

stack-mou *n* peat-dust and broken peat found at peat-stacks.

staddle *n* the lower part of a corn-stack as far as the sides are upright; a small temporary stack.

staig *n* a young horse, one, two, or three years old, not yet broken for riding or work.

stair-pit *n* a coal-pit in which the miners could descend or ascend by a ladder erected from top to bottom in short lengths.

stale *n* the foundation on which a rick or stack is placed.

stalf-hirdit *n* applied to a flock or herd under the care of a shepherd.

stamp-coil, -cole *n* a small rick of hay.

stane-bark *n* liverwort, a lichen yielding a purple dye.

stannyel, stane-horse *n* a stallion.

staneraw *n* the rock-liverwort, a lichen producing a purple dye.

staners, stanners *n* the gravelly shores of a river.

stank-bree *n* the edge of a pool; the brow of a ditch.

stanked, stankit *adj* surrounded by a ditch.

stannery *adj* gravelly.

starn, stern, sternyt *n, adj* a star; starry.

starn-light *n* the light of the stars.

starnie *n* a little star.

startle *v* to run wildly about, as cows do in hot weather.

stead, steading, steddyng, steeding *n* the ground on which a house stands, or the vestiges of a former building; a farm-house and offices.

steak-raid *n* that portion of the live stock, taken in predatory incursion, which was supposed to belong to any proprietor through whose land the prey was driven.

stede, steid *n, v* place; to place.

steekin-slap *n* a gap with a gate opening and shutting.

steel *n* a wooded *cleugh*, or precipice, greater than a *slain*; the lower part of a ridge projecting from a hill, where the ground declines on each side.

steen *n* a spring.

steep-grass *n* the butterwort.

steering-fur *v* a slight ploughing.

stein, sten *n* a stone.

steinie-gate *n* the place where stones, gathered off the fields, are collected.

steiny *adj* stony.

stell *n, adj* a covert; a shelter; an enclosure for cattle, higher than a common fold; a deep pool in a river, where nets for catching salmon are placed; steep.

stellage *n* (perhaps) the ground on which a fair or market is held.

stepping *n* a way; a path.

sterk, stirk *n* a young ox or heifer.

stern-licht *n* starlight.

sternyt *adj* starry.

stertlin *adj* a term primarily used to denote the restlessness of cattle, in consequence of the bite of the *cleg* or gad-fly, or even of their hearing the sound of its approach as they immediately run for shelter, as in "ma kye are aw stertlin the day, that I canna keep them i' the park".

steug *n* a thorn; anything sharp pointed.

stibble-lea, -field, -land *n* a stubble field.

stibblewin *v* (applied to a ridge of corn) cut down before another, the one cut down being between that other and the standing corn.

stibbler *n* a horse turned loose after harvest into the stubble; a labourer in harvest who goes from ridge to ridge, cutting and gathering the handfuls left by those who in their reaping go regularly forward.

stichle *v* to rustle.

sticking-bull *n* a horned bull in the habit of attacking people.

stiggy *n* a stile, or passage over a wall; a stair; a flight of steps.

stile *n* a sparred gate.

stimpart, stimpert *n* quarter of a peck; (used of ground) as much as will produce a quarter peck of flax-seed; a young person who can barely *shear* out the fourth part of a ridge; an unskillful *shearer*.

stinking Davies *n* the common ragwort.

stinking Elshander *n* the common tansy.

stinking Roger *n* figwort.

stinking-weed, -willie *n* the common ragwort.

stir *v* to plough slightly.

stirring-furrow *n* the second ploughing across the first; the seed-furrow.

stitch *n* a furrow or drill, as of turnips, potatoes etc.

stock and brock *phr* the whole of one's property, including what is properly called stock, and that consists of such articles as are not *entire*.

stoddart, stoddert *n* a grassy hollow among hills.

stog *n, v* (applied to reaping) the stubble which is left too high, or an inequality thus produced; a piece of decayed tree standing out of the ground; to cut down grain so as to leave some of the stubble too high; to push a stick down through the soil, in order to ascertain its depth.

stole *n* a stalk of corn.

stoll *n* a place of safety.

stone-lands *n* tenement houses built of stone.

stoo *v* to crop.

stook *n* a shock of corn, consisting of twelve sheaves.

stookie *n* a small stook of corn; a bullock that has horns like those of a goat.

stooky-Sunday *n* the Sunday in harvest on which the greatest number of stooks is seen in the field.

stool-bent *n* moss-rush.

stot *n* a young bull or ox.

stouff, stuff *n* dust.

stour *n* dust; dust in motion; a finely driven snow.

stowins *n* the tender blades or sprouts from colewort or any other vegetable.

strabs *n* any withered vegetable loosely scattered abroad, or any light rubbish blown about by the wind, or lying about in a dispersed state.

strae-kiln *n* a kiln dug in the face of a hillock, and roofed with pieces of trees covered with drawn straw, on which corn was put, a fire being lighted in front, with openings at the back to draw the heat.

strag *n* a thin growing crop, the stalks straggling.

straict *n* a narrow pass.

straik *n, v* a tract of country; ground traversed; the strip of ground passed over at one turn in harrowing; the act of travelling over a tract of land.

straik o' day, straikin o' daylicht, streeking o' day *phr* daybreak; dawn of day.

strait bields *n* a shelter formed by a steep hill.

strath *n* a valley of considerable extent, through which a river runs; a country confined by hills on two sides of a river.

streamers *n* the Aurora Borealis.

streamoury *adj* having streams of light from the Aurora Borealis.

streaw *n* the shrew mouse.

strekin *v* (used of ploughing) drawing the first furrows at the beginning of spring.

stremouris *n* streams of light; Aurora Borealis.

strife rigs, striferiggs *n* debatable ground; patches of land common to all.

striking-teck *v* the cutting of heather with a short scythe.

strip *n* a long, narrow plantation or belt of trees.

strone *n* a hill that terminates a range; the end of a ridge.

strow *n* a shrew-mouse.

stubble-rig *n* a stubble-field.

studderts *n* grassy patches on hillsides, or between hills where there is a fresh spring of water.

stug *n* a thorn or prickle, as in "I've gotten a stug i' my fit", I have got a thorn in my foot; a piece of decayed tree standing out of the ground.

stug *v* to shear unequally, so as to leave part of the stubble higher than the rest

stuggy *adj* (applied to stubble) of unequal length, in consequence of carelessness in cutting down the corn.

sturdy *n* a plant which grows amongst corn, which, when eaten, causes giddiness and torpidity.

sturtle *v* (used of cattle) to run about wildly in hot weather.

sucken *n, v* the territory subjected to a certain jurisdiction; legally astricted; those who are bound to have their corn ground at a certain mill are said to be *sucken* to it.

suckies, suckie clover *n* the flowers of clover.

suggie *adj* wet land; wet, marshy, boggy, as in "moist, suggie lan'".

suggie *n* a young sow.

suilye, sulye, soilye, sullige *n* soil; ground; country.

sumer *n* a sumpter-horse.

summer, simmer *v* to feed cattle etc. during summer.

sun-dew webs *n* gossamer.

sunny-side, sunny half *adj* a description of the position of land, denoting its southern exposure, as contradistinguished from that which lies in the shade.

surrock *n* the sorrel.

susk *n* loose straw, rubbish.

suthart *adj, adv* southward, southern.

swail *n* a gentle rising in the ground with a corresponding declivity.

swailsh *n* a part of a mountain that slopes much, or any part of the face of the hill which is not so steep as the rest.

swaultie *n* a fat animal.

swap *n* the husk of peas before the peas are formed; the peas themselves, in the pod, while yet in an immature state.

swap *v* (applied to peas and other leguminous herbs) beginning to have pods.

swar *n* a snare.

sware *n* the declination of a mountain or hill, near the summit; the most level spot between two hills.

swarfe *n* the surface.

swarth *n* sward; the surface of the ground.

swash *v, n* the noise made in falling upon the ground.

sway *n* the line of grass as it falls from the scythe or mowing-machine.

swee *n* a line of grass cut down by the mower.

swell *n* a bog.

sweet-cicely *n* the great chervil.

sweet-gale *n* the bog-myrtle.

sweet-mary *n* the rosemary.

swile *n* a bog in a meadow.

swine-arnuts *n* tall oat grass with tuberous roots.

swine-thistle *n* the sow-thistle.

swine's mosscorts *n* clown's all-heal.

swoon *adj* corn is "in the swoon" when, although the strength of the seed is exhausted, the plant has not fairly struck root. In this state the blade appears sickly and faded.

sword *n* the leaf of the common yellow iris.

swyle *n* a bog.

swylie *adj* full of bogs.

swyre *n* the descent of a hill; the pass between two hills.

sye *n* the herb called chives; the small wild onion; a scythe.

T

taatie *n* a potato.

tabrach *n* animal food nearly in a state of carrion.

tade *n* the sheep-louse; the tick.

tae-breeth *adv, adj, prep* the smallest possible distance.

taff-dyke *n* a fence made of turf.

taftan *n* a toft; a homestead.

tag *v* (applied to the moon) to wane, as in "the mune's taggin'".

taghairm *n* a form of divination formerly used in the Highlands.

taid *v* to manure land by the droppings from cattle, either in pasturing or folding.

taid *n* a toad.

taid-stule *n* a mushroom. *See also* paddie-stule.

taiggie, taggit, taigie, tygie *n* a cow which has the point of the tail white.

tailwind *n* "to shear wi'a tail-wind", to reap or cut the grain, not straight across the ridge, but diagonally.

tailor's-gartens *n* ribbon grass.

tainchell *n, v* a mode of catching deer.

taing *n* a flat tongue of land projecting into the sea.

taith *n* the dung of pastured sheep or cattle; a tuft of grass growing where dung has been dropped in a field.

tak wi' *v* (as applied to the vegetable kingdom) to begin to sprout or to take root; it is said that "corn has not tane wi'", when it has not sprung up; a tree is said to be beginning to "tak wi'" when it begins to take root.

tammock *n* a hillock.

tandle *n* a bonfire.

tangle *n* an icicle.

tap-rung *n* the highest point; summit.

tap-swarm *n* the first swarm which a hive of bees casts off.

tarn *n* a mountain lake.

tas, tass *n* a small heap of earth; a cluster of flowers.

tath *v* to make a field produce grass in rank tufts by the application of any manure.

tath-faud *n* a fold in which cattle

are shut up during night, for the purpose of manuring the ground with their dung.

tathing *n* a raising of rank grass by manure.

tatie, tattie, tawtie *n* a vulgar name for a potato.

taw *n* a streak of light.

tawtie-bogle *n* a scare-crow.

teak *n* the otter.

teep *n* a ram.

teil, tele *v* to cultivate the soil.

teleland *n* arable land.

thair-doun *adv* downwards.

thair-east *adj, adv, n* in the east; towards the east.

thairfra, thairfrae *prep* from that place.

thairfurth *adj, adv, prep* in the open air.

the-furth *adj, adv, prep* out of doors, abroad.

thill *n* a coarse subsoil of gravel and clay.

thimble, thimmel *n* the harebell.

thinter *n* a three year old sheep.

thirl *n* (used of land) in which tenants are bound to bring all their grain to a certain mill.

thirlestane-grass *n* saxifrage.

thoft *n* a toft; homestead; messuage.

thoftin' *n* a *thoft*, the house built upon a toft; the using and right of such house.

thorter *v* to cross the furrow in ploughing; to harrow a field across the ridges.

thoumart *n* the polecat.

thrave, threave *n* twenty four sheaves of grain; a large quantity of people; a crowd; to work by *thraves* in a harvest and to be paid accordingly.

thraver *n* a reaper paid according to the *thraves* he cuts down.

thraw-mouse *n* the shrew-mouse.

three-fold *n* the bog-bean.

threuch-stane, throch-stane, through, thruch, thrugh *n* a flat tombstone.

thrinter *n* a sheep of three winters.

thrissill, thrisle *n* the thistle.

thristly *adj* abounding in thistles; bristly.

through-gang *n* a thoroughfare; a passage.

thrunter *n* a ewe in her fourth year.

thulmard, thumart, thum- mart *n* the polecat.

thumbles *n* round-leaved bell flowers; harebells.

thunder-and-lightning *n* the common lung-wort.

thunder-flower *n* the common red poppy.

tike, tyke, tyk *n* a dog; a cur, properly one of a larger and common breed.

timty *v* a method of digging the ground and covering it with *sea-ware* in the Isle of Lewis.

tinchell *n* a circle of sportsmen, who, by surrounding a great space, and gradually narrowing, brought great quantities of deer together; a trap or a snare.

ting *n* a tongue of land jutting into the sea; (used of cattle) to swell up through eating clover, etc.

tip *n* a ram.

tirlie *n* a winding in a footpath; *tirlies,* little circular stoppages in path-ways, which turn round.

tod *n* the fox.

tod-hole, tod's-hole *n* a hole in which the fox hides himself.

tod-touzing *v* the Scottish method of hunting the fox, by shouting, bustling, guarding, hallooing etc.

tod-track *n* the traces of the fox's feet in snow – by the marks of his feet, he seems to have but two, for he sets his hind feet exactly in the tracks of the fore ones.

tod-tyke *n* a mongrel between a fox and a dog.

tod's-tails *n* alpine club-moss, a herb.

todler-tyke *n* a kind of bumble-bee.

toft *n* a bed for plants of cabbage etc.; land once tilled and now abandoned.

toft-field *n* a field belonging to a toft or messuage.

tolling *v* the sound emitted by a queen bee before swarming.

tommack *n* a hillock.

toman *n* a hillock; a mound; a thicket.

tomminaul *n* an ox or heifer a year old.

tomshee *n* a fairy hillock.

toopikin, toopick, toopichan, toopichen, topick *n* a pinnacle; a summit; a narrow pile raised so high as to be in danger of falling.

toor, tour *n* a turf or peat; a weed.

tor, tore, torr *n* a high hill, a high rock.

torrie *n* a beetle that breeds in dung, and consumes grain.

touch-spale, touchbell *n* the earwig.

touk *n* an embankment to hinder the water from washing away the soil.

toum *n* the gossamer.

toun, town *n* town, city; also

a farmer's steading or a small collection of dwelling-houses; a farmstead.

towerick, towrickie *n* a summit or any thing elevated, especially if on an eminence.

towling *n* the signal given, in a hive, for some time before the bees swarm.

towmondall *n* a yearling.

trankle *n* a small rick of hay.

transe *n* a passage.

trantle *n* the rut made by a cart-wheel when it is deep.

trantle-hole *n* a place into which odd or broken things are thrown.

tras *n* the track of game.

trinkie *n* a narrow channel between rocks on the sea-coast.

trogue *n* a young horse.

trouble *n* a name given by miners to a sudden break in the stratum of coal.

troush *n* a call to cattle, as in "troush, hawkie".

trow *n* "the trow of the water", the lower ground through which a river runs.

trysting-place *n* the appointed place for a meeting.

tryst-stane *n* a stone anciently erected for marking out a rendezvous.

trysting-style *n* a stile at which lovers meet.

tuack *n* a small hillock; a little hill or mole-hill.

tuck *n* a jetty on the side of a river.

tuggin *n* the beech or stone marten.

tulipase *n* a tulip.

tulloch *n* a hillock.

tump *n* a small mound or hillock.

tumult *n* the land attached to a cottar's house.

tup, tupe *n* the ram.

turven, turvven *n* peats.

tushalagy *n* the *Tussilago* or coltsfoot.

tushy-lucky-gowan *n* the coltsfoot.

tushloch, tuschlich *n* a small bundle or truss; a small cock of hay, straw, etc.

tusk *v* to cut peat from above.

twa-horse farm *n* a farm requiring two horses to work it.

twinter *n* a beast that is two years old.

tyme *n* the herb thyme.

U

ubit *n* a hairy caterpillar.

ui *n* an isthmus or neck of land.

ule o' heat *phr, n* the mist that rises from the ground in a hot day.

ullier *n* the water that runs through a dunghill.

uncorn *n* wild oats.

uncover *n* to drive a fox out of cover.

under-fur sowing *v* sowing in a shallow furrow.

undern *n* the third hour of the artificial day, according to the ancient reckoning, i.e. nine o'clock.

undernight *adj* under cloud of night; by night.

up-a-land *adv, prep, adj* at a distance from the sea; in the country; rustic.

upsun *adv* after sunrise; "it was upsun", the sun was not set.

uplands, up of land, upon-land, up-plane *n* one who lives in the country as distinguished from the town.

upright bur *n* the fir-moss, *Lycopodium selago.*

upwith *n* an ascent; a rising ground.

urchin *n* a hedgehog.

ure *n* a denomination of land; soil; a bad soil, a kind of coloured haze, which the sun-beams make in the summer time, in the passing through that moisture which the sun exhales from the land and ocean., as in "an ill ure".

ureen *n* a ewe.

V

vane *n, v* a call to a horse to come near.

veil *n* a calf.

veir, ver, vere *n* the spring.

venter *n* anything driven ashore by tide or wind.

verge *n* a belt or stripe of planting.

vestrean *n* the west.

voar, vor, vour *n* the spring; seed-time.

vole-mouse *n* the short-tailed mouse, or field-mouse.

vord *n* a high hill.

vung *v* to move swiftly with a buzzing or humming sound.

W

wa-gang crap *n* the last crop before the tenant quits his farm.

wab *n* a web.

wachie *adj* wet; foggy; swampy.

waggle *n* a bog; a marsh.

waile *n* a vale or valley.

wair, ware *n* the spring.

wake-robin *n* the *Arum maculatum*. Some bakers in Teviotdale are said to use this as a charm against witchcraft.

wald *n* the plain; the ground; yellow weed; dyer's weed, *Reseda luteola*.

wale *n* a well; a fountain; the verge of a mountain.

wallan *v* to wither; to fade.

wall-girse, wall-girse-kail *n* watercress

wallowit *adj* withered.

waly, waly-sprig *n* a small flower.

wandocht *n* a weak or puny creature.

wane *n* a habitation.

wanearthlie *adj* not belonging to this world; preternatural.

war-brook *n* a large heap of seaweed cast ashore.

ward, waird *n* a division of a county; a piece of pasture; land enclosed on all sides for young animals; a beacon-hill, a signal-hill; confinement.

ware-bear *n* barley raised by means of seaweed.

waretyme *n* the season of spring; early period of life.

wared *adj* manured with seaweed.

Warlock-craigie *n* a wizards' rock.

warlock-knowe *n* a hill where wizards were thought to meet.

warp *v* (used of bees) to take flight.

warset *n* a dog employed by a thief for watching deer.

warsh-crop *n* a name given to the third crop from *outfield*.

wart *n* the top of a high hill, or a tumulus or mound thrown up on high ground in the Orkney and Shetland Islands, for the purpose of conveying intelligence.

wastege *n* a place of desolation.

wastland *n* the west country.

wastle *adv, adj* to the westward of.

water-fur *v* to form furrows in ploughed ground for draining off the water.

water-purpie *n* common brook-lime, a herb.

water-shed *n* the highest ground in any part of a country, from which rivers descend in opposite directions.

water-slain moss *n* peat-earth carried off by water and afterwards deposited.

water-tath *n* luxuriant grass proceeding from excess of moisture.

waterkyle *n* meadow-ground possessed by the tenants of an estate by rotation.

watling street, vatlant streit *n* a term used to denote the milky way, from its fancied resemblance to a broad street or causeway.

wauchie *adj* swampy.

wauld, wald *n* the plain open country, without wood.

way-gaun, wa'-gaun, way-going *v* removing from a farm or habitation.

webis, weebis, weebie, weebo *n* the common ragwort.

weedock *n* a little weed.

weem *n* a natural cave.

weeuk *v* a term used to denote the squeaking of rats, the neighing of stallions, or the bellowing of bulls when they raise their voices to the shrillest pitch.

weir-buse *n* a partition between cows.

weist *n* the west.

wessel *adj, adv* westward.

wham *n* a wide and flat glen, usually applied to one through which a brook runs.

whatrick *n* a weasel.

whaum *n* a hollow part of a field; (perhaps) "a glen where the ground on both sides spreads out into an ample bosom of hills"; (perhaps) a hollow in one hill or mountain.

wheeliecruse *n* a churchyard.

whezle *n* the weasel.

whiddie *n* a name for a hare.

whihe *n, v* the sound of an adder, her *fuffing* noise when angered.

whink *n, v* a term used to denote the bark of a collie, when, from want of breath, he is unable to extend his cry, or his shrill impatient tone, when he loses sight of the hare which he has been pursuing.

whinnerin' *adj* "a whinnerin' drouth", a severe drought, accompanied with a sifting wind; it is applied to any thing so much dried, in consequence of extreme drought, as to rustle to the touch, as in "the corn's a whinnerin".

whip aff, whip awa *v* to fly off with velocity; to be rapidly carried upwards and downwards; to move briskly.

white hare *n* the alpine hare.

whittret, whutterick *n* the weasel.

whutterick-fuffing *n* a gathering of weasels.

whuttle-grass *n Melilot trifolium*, called also King's-claver.

why *n, v* a call to a cart-horse to keep to the left.

wick *n* a farmstead.

wide-gab *n* the fishing frog.

wight *n* the shrew-mouse.

wilcat, wildcat *n* the polecat.

wild-cotton *n* the tassel cotton-grass.

wild-liquorice *n* the sweet milk-vetch.

wild-pink *n* the maiden pink.

wildfire *n* the phosphorescence of decaying vegetation etc; summer lightning; a will o' the wisp; the small spearmint; the marsh-marigold.

will-kail *n* wild mustard or charlock.

willcorn *n* wild oats growing without cultivation.

win *v* to dwell; to dry corn, hay, peats etc. by exposing them to the air; often used to denote harvest-making in general; to raise from a quarry; to work a mine of any kind.

wine-berry *n* the common

currant.

wine-tree *n* the blackthorn.

winnail *n* a windmill.

winter *v* to pasture cattle etc. through the winter.

winter-haining *n* the preserving of grass from being fed on during the winter.

winter-hap *n* winter covering.

winterer *n* a horse, sheep or cow kept to pasture in a particular place during winter.

wirry-cow *n* a bug-bear; a scarecrow; a goblin; the devil.

wisen *v* to wither; to become dry and hard.

witch *n* a moth.

witch-bell *n* the harebell.

witch-bracken *n* a species of bracken.

witch-gowan *n* the dandelion.

witches' butterfly *n* a large, thick bodied moth, of drab or light-brown colour.

witches' knots *n* a sort of matted bunches, resembling the nests of birds, frequently seen on stunted thorns or birches; a disease supposed to be produced by a stoppage of the juices.

witches'-thimbles, -thummles *n* the flowers of the fox-glove.

wither-gloom *n* the clear sky near the horizon.

wither-lands *adj, adv, prep* against the sun's course.

withershins *adj, adv, prep* in the contrary direction, properly, contrary to the course of the sun.

withershins-grow *n* anything growing contrary to the sun's course.

witherspail *n* goosegrass or clivers, *Galium aparine.*

witter-stone *n* (perhaps) a stone originally placed as a *witter*, or mark.

wizards, wizzards *n* quick-grass, or other weeds, dried or *wizzened* on fallow fields.

wizzen *v* to become dry.

wob *n* a web.

won *adj* raised from a quarry, also dug from a mine.

won *v* to dwell.

wonner *n* a dweller.

wonnyng, wyning *n* a dwelling.

wonyeonis *n* onions.

worm-month *n* a designation given to the month of July, from the hatching of many kind of reptiles in this month.

worm-web *n* a spider's web.

worri-cow *n* a scarecrow.

wort *v* to dig up.

woubit *n* a hairy worm; one of those worms which appear as if covered with wool.

wouch, wouff *n, v* the bark of a dog; to bark.

wouf *n* a wolf.

wra *n* a hiding-place; a lurking hole.

wrachys *n* ghosts.

wrack *n* dog's grass, *Gramen caninum*; couch grass, *Triticum repens*.

wrang-gaites *adj, adv, prep* in the wrong direction; against the course of the sun.

wread, wreath *n* a place for enclosing cattle.

wudwise *n* a yellow flower which grows on bad land and has a bitter taste.

wuggle *n* a bog or marsh.

wullcat *n* a wild cat.

wybis *n* the common ragwort; the tansy.

wynan *n* the half of a field.

wynd *n* an alley; a lane.

wynd *v* to separate from the chaff; to dry by exposing to the air.

wyndel-stray *n* smooth-crested grass; a withered stalk of grass, standing where it grew.

wyver *n* a weaver; a spider.

wyver's-wobs *n* cobwebs.

X, Y, Z

yad, yaud *n* an old mare; a worn out horse.

yaikert *adj* (used of grain) eared.

yarr *n* spurry, a weed found in poor land.

yattle *n, adj* a quantity of small stones on the land; (applied to ground) covered with small stones.

yauvins *n* the beards of corn.

yavil *n* the second crop after lea.

year-auld *n* a colt one year old; a young bullock or heifer.

yearock *n* a hen one year old, or that has just begun to lay eggs.

yellowing-grass *n* a grass yielding a yellow dye.

yerd, yird, yirth *n* earth; soil.

yerd-fast *adj* firmly fastened to the

ground.

yerd-meal *n* earth-mould; church-yard dust.

yethert *adj* heather-clad.

yield of the day *phr* the influence of the sun on frost.

yird *v* to bury.

yird-fast *n* a stone well fastened in the ground; *yird-fasts*, large stones sticking in the *yird*, or earth, that the plough cannot move.

yird-laigh *adj* as low as earth.

yirdie-bee *n* a bee that burrows in the ground.

yirdlins *adj, adv* to the earth, earthwards.

yirlich *adj* wild; unnatural.

Yorkshire fog *n* the meadow soft-grass.

youth-wort *n* the common sun-dew.

yowie *n* a little ewe.

yule-blinker *n* the North Star.

Part two

Wood

A

aar *n* the alder.

aik *n* the oak.

aik-snag *n* the broken bough of an oak.

aiken *adj* of or belonging to oak.

aiten *n* the juniper.

aixman *n* a hewer of wood.

aix-tre *n* an axle-tree.

alar *adj* of or belonging to the alder-tree.

alar, aller, arn, alrone *n* the alder.

alars yet *n* (perhaps) the gate overspread with alder.

apple-glory *n* apple blossom.

Arbroath pippen *n* the name of an apple.

ashen *adj* belonging to, or consisting of, ash-trees.

ash-keys *n* the seed vessel of the ash.

auchindoras *n* a large thorn-tree at the end of a house.

auwis-bore *n* the circular vacuity left in a piece of wood, from a knot coming out of it. According to vulgar tradition, this orifice has been made by the fairies.

awmous-dish *n* the wooden dish in which mendicants receive their *alms*, when given in meat.

awte *n* the direction in which a stone or piece of wood splits; the grain.

B

backs *n* the outermost boards from a sawn tree.

backet *n* a box or trough of wood to carry fuel, ashes, etc.; a small wooden box with a sloping lid, fastened by leather bands, to keep the salt dry. It is generally called the *saut-backet*.

backie, baikie *n* a square wooden vessel for holding food for cattle, fuel, ashes, etc.

bait *n* the grain or cleavage of wood or stone.

bark *v* to strip a tree of its bark, especially for the purpose of tanning.

barkit *adj* stripped of the bark.

bass *n* the inner bark of a tree

bat *v* (used of mistletoe, ivy, etc.) to cling to a tree, grow on a tree.

bauk, bawk *n* a cross beam; a rafter; a strip of land left unploughed two or three feet in length.

beetle *n* a flat piece of wood used by dyers and washerwomen

beyr-tree *n* the bier on which a corpse is carried to the grave.

belt(in) *n* a clump or line of trees, often used to denote a strip of planting.

beltie *n* a small, narrow plantation.

bewis *n* boughs.

beuch *n* a bough; a branch of a tree.

bicker *n* a bowl or dish for containing liquor, properly, one made of wood.

bield *n* (used of trees) a shelter, as in "everyman bows to the bush he gets bield frae".

birk, birkin tree *n* birch.

birk-knowe *n* a knoll covered in birches.

birken *adj* abounding with birches

birkinshaw *n* a small wood consisting mainly of birches.

black wood *n* ebony.

blae *n* the rough parts of wood left after boring or sawing.

blade *n* a leaf.

blaze *n* the mark made by an axe slicing off bark from a tree, normally done to indicate the tree is to be felled.

bleeze *n* the rough parts of wood left after boring or sawing.

blunk *n* a small block of wood or stone; a dull lifeless person.

boardtree *n* a term used for the plank on which a corpse is stretched.

boil, bole *n* the trunk of a tree.

bonnet fir *n* Scots pine.

boogers, bougers *n* rafters.

boortree, bourtree, bore tree *n* elder tree.

borral *n* elder tree.

bossie *n* a large wooden basin, used for oatmeal in baking.

boughtie *n* a twig.

bountree *n* the elder.

bountree-berries *n* the fruit of the elder, from which elderberry wine is made.

bountry-gun *n* a small air gun made of a twig of an elder with the pith taken out; a pellet of wet paper being forced up the tube and another put in and pushed up towards it, the compressed air between the two forces out the first with an explosion.

bousy, bowsie, bouzy *adj* bushy, wooded.

brawlins *n* the trailing strawberry tree.

brondyn *adj* branched.

bronys *n* branches, boughs.

browl *n* a gnarled limb of a tree.

browls *n* bits of dry wood gathered for burning.

buck *n* the beech tree.

buise *v* (perhaps) to swing, to be hanged, as in "to shoot the buise".

bullister *n* sloe-bush; the wild plum tree.

bur *n* the cones of the fir.

burden-carrier *n* a carrier of wood.

burn-wood *n* firewood.

burrel, burrell *n* a hollow piece of wood used in twisting rope.

busk *n* a bush.

buss *n* a thicket; a clump or stand of trees; a wood; a bush.

bussie *adj* bushy.

C

caber *n* a long slender tree trunk, pole; a large, heavy pole for tossing at athletics competitions; a beam, a rafter, a large stick; a rung.

calchen *n* a square frame of wood, with ribs across it in the form of a gridiron, in which *fir-candles* are dried in the chimney.

cammel *n* a crooked piece of

wood, used as a hook for hanging anything on.

camrel *n* a crooked piece of wood, passed through the ankle of a sheep, or other animal, by means of which it is suspended til it can be flayed and disemboweled.

cannle fir *n* split fir-wood used instead of candles.

cappie *adj* given to warping, like green wood.

carf *n* a cut in timber for insertion of another piece of wood, the incision made by an axe or saw.

cashie *adj* (applied to vegetables and the shoots of trees) luxuriant and succulent.

cauld-bark *n* a coffin; a grave.

chaveling, shoveling *n, v* a tool especially employed by cartwrights and coachmakers, for smoothing hollow or circular wood.

chow *n* a wooden ball used in shinty.

claar *n* a large wooden chest.

claff *n* the cleft or part of a tree where the branches separate.

clamsh *n* a piece of wood with which a thing is clumsily mended.

clawscrunt *n* an old tree against which cattle rub themselves.

cliftiness *adj* the quality of being easily kindled, including that of burning brightly.

clivvie *n* a cleft in the branch of a tree; an artificial cleft in a piece of wood for holding a rush-light.

clod-mell *n* a wooden mallet for breaking the clods of the field, especially on clayey ground, before harrowing it.

cloff *n* a cleft or branches of a tree.

clog, clogge *n* a small short log; a short cut of a tree; a thick piece of timber.

clowg *n* a small bar of wood, fixed to the door-post in the middle by a screw-nail, round which it moves, so that either end of it may be turned round over the end of the door, to keep it closed.

clupper *n* a wooden saddle.

cockie-bendie *n* the cone of a fir tree; the large conical buds of the plane-tree.

cog *n* a hollow wooden vessel of a circular form for holding milk, broth, etc.

cogie, coggie *n* a small wooden dish.

coglan-tree, covin-tree *n* the large tree in front of an old Scottish mansion where the laird met his visitors.

conter-tree *n* cross bar of wood, a stick attached by a piece of rope to a door, and resting on the wall on each side, thus keeping the door shut from without.

coom *n* the wooden frame used in building a bridge; the lid of a coffin, from it being arched.

cootie *n* a wooden kitchen dish; a small wooden shaped bowl; a bucket shaped barrel.

cow *n* a twig or branch; used to denote a bush; a besom made of broom.

cowt *n* a strong stick; a rung.

crook-studie, -tree *n* a cross beam in a chimney from which the crook is suspended.

cruban *n* a wooden pannier fixed on a horse's back.

cuchil *n* a forest or grove.

cups and ladles *n* the husks of an acorn, from their resemblance to these utensils.

curl-doddy *n* the cone of a pine or fir-tree.

currack *n* a small cart made of twigs.

cuthil, cuthil *n* a forest or grove.

cutwiddie *n* the piece of wood by which a harrow is fastened to a yolk.

CURL-DODDIES

D

dais'd *adj* (used of wood) beginning to lose its proper colour and texture.

daised *adj* (used of wood, plants, etc.) spoiled, withered, rotten.

dale *n* a plank; a board for measuring a corpse.

dall *n* a large cake made of sawdust and mixed with the dung of cows, used by poor people for fuel.

dead-chack *n* the sound of woodworm in a house, regarded as an omen of death.

dean, den *n* a deeply wooded valley.

dedechack *n* the sound made by a woodworm in houses, so called from its clicking noise, and because vulgarly supposed to be a premonition of death; also called *chackie-mill* because of resemblance to the sound of a mill; the dinner prepared for the magistrates of a borough after a public execution.

ding *v* to cut bark up in small pieces for the tanner.

dog-rowan-tree *n* the red elder.

dogs *n* pieces of iron, having a zig-zag form, for fixing a tree in the saw-pit, so denominated, (perhaps), from keeping hold as dogs do with their teeth.

dool-tree *n* a gallows; a tree or post on which evil-doers were hanged in the exercise of the power of 'pit and gallows'; a tree which marks the goal in playing ball.

douk *n* a wooden wedge driven into a wall.

duddie *n* a dish turned out of solid wood, having two ears, and which is, generally, of an octagonal form on the brim. This is different from a *luggie*.

dugeon-tre, dudgeon *n* wood for staves.

E

easer *n* maple-wood.

eizel, aizle, isil, isel *n* a hot ember, wood reduced to the state of charcoal; in plural, a metaphor for the ruins of a country desolated by war.

elf-bore *n* a hole in a piece of wood, out of which a knot has dropped, or been driven (viewed by the superstitious as the operation of the fairies).

elf-mill *n* the sound made by woodworm, viewed by the vulgar as preternatural.

eller *n* the elder.

esch *n* the ash.

eschin *adj* belonging to the ash.

etnagh, etnach *adj* of or belonging to the juniper.

etnagh berries *n* juniper berries.

ezar *n* maple-wood, of or belonging to the maple.

F

fadge *n* a bundle of sticks.

fagald *n* a bundle of twigs or heather tied with straw ropes, formerly used for shutting up the doorway under night, when there was no door.

fir candle *n* a torch; firwood used as a candle; a splinter from a moss-fallen fir tree, used as a light.

fir-dale *n* a plank of fir.

fir-fecket *n* a coffin.

fir-futtle *n* a large knife used for splitting *candle-fir*.

fir-gown, fir-jacket *n* a coffin.

fir-yowe *n* a fir cone.

firth *n* a small wood.

firrin, firron *adj* of or belonging to the fir or the pine tree.

firwood *n* bogwood, formerly used for candles.

fit-tree *n* the treadle of a spinning-wheel.

fleasocks *n* the shavings of wood.

fleech *v* (used of a carpenter) to shave off spills in planing wood.

fleuris *n* blossom.

flingin-tree *n* a piece of timber used as a partition between horses; a flail, the lower part of a flail.

flouncing *v* (used of trees in a gale) tossing to and fro.

flurish, flourish *v* blossom.

forstaris *n* a female inhabitant of a forest.

freuch, freugh *adj* (used of wood) brittle; (used of corn) dry.

frith *n* a wood; a clearing in a wood.

G

gab-stick *n* a wooden spoon.

gaberts *n* a kind of gallows for supporting the wheel of a draw-well; three poles of wood forming an angle at the top, for weighing hay.

gag, gaig, geg *n* a rent or crack in wood.

gail, gale *v* (applied to inanimate objects, as unseasoned wood) to break into chinks.

gean-tree *n* wild cherry tree.

gell *n* a crack or rent in wood.

glack *n* an opening in a wood, where the wind comes with force; that part of a tree where a bough branches out.

goan *n* a wooden dish for meat.

gnarr *n* a hard knot in wood

grain *n* a branch; an offshoot of a tree.

grist *n* size, measurement, texture, thickness of anything, grain of wood etc.

gruel-tree *n* a porridge-stick; a spurtle.

gurly *adj* (applied to trees) gnarled.

gurr *n* a knotty stick or tree.

gymmer *n* evergreen.

H

hag *n, v* a portion of a wood marked for felling; brushwood; felled wood used for fuel, the less branches used for fire-wood, after the trees are felled for carpenter-work; to hack, cut, chop wood; to cut down trees, prepare timber.

hagberry *n* the bird-cherry.

hag-wood *n* a copse wood fitted for having a regular cutting of trees.

hagger *n* one who uses a hatchet; one employed to cut down trees.

hagman *n* a feller of wood, one who gains his sustenance by cutting and selling wood.

handie *n* a milking pail; a wooden dish for holding food. It seems thus denominated because it has an ear or hand for holding. *See also* luggie.

hangarell *n* a piece of wood on which bridles, halters are hung.

hard-tree *n* hardwood; close-grained timber.

haw-buss, haw-tree *n* the hawthorn bush.

hawkathraw *n* a country carpenter.

hazel-shaw *n* an abrupt flat piece of ground at the bottom of a hill, covered in hazels.

heben-wood *n* ebony.

herding-tree *n* a herd-boy's stick.

herne-shaw *n* a shaw or wood where herons breed.

hiddie-giddie *n* a short piece of wood with a sharp point at each end, fixed on the trace for keeping horses or oxen apart in ploughing.

hirst *n* a resting-place; a small eminence on a rising ground; a small wood.

hizzle *n* a hazel tree.

hoburn sauch *n* the laburnum.

hochimes, hougham *n* bent pieces of wood, slung on each side of a horse, for supporting dung panniers.

hog trees *v* to make pollards; to cut them over about the place where the branches begin to divide, in this case they are said to be *hoggit.*

holene, hollen, holyn *n* the holly tree.

holland *n* of or belonging to the holly.

holt, hout *n* a wooded hill; a wood.

I

image *n* a wooded figure carved by the fairies in the likeness of a person intended to be stolen.

janker *n* a long pole, on two wheels, used for carrying wood, the log being fixed to it by strong clasps.

jeest, jest *n* a joist.

jigger *n* a vehicle for carrying trees from a wood; a *janker.*

jow, jowie *n* a fir cone.

K

kabe *n* a thowl or strong pin of wood for keeping an oar steady.

kempel *v* to cut wood into billets.

kendlin-wood *n* matchwood, splinters or chips of wood for lighting fires.

kennelling *n* firewood.

keoch *n* a wooded glen.

key *n* the seed of the ash.

keysart *n* a hack, or frame of wood in which cheeses are hung up for being dried.

kind gallows *n* a designation given to the fatal tree at Crieff.

kink *n* a bend in the bole of a tree.

kipple *n* a rafter.

kipple-fit *n* the lower part of a rafter.

knag *n* a knot or spur projecting from a tree.

knaggie *adj* (used of wood) full of knots.

knap *n* some sort of wooden vessel.

knappers *n* the mast of oak etc.

knarlie *adj* knotty.

knaur *n* a knot in wood.

knool *n* a wooden pin fixed in the end of a halter for holding by.

knurr *n* a knot of wood, a round knotty projection on a tree; the wooden ball used in shinty; anything small or stunted in growth.

L

land *n* an open space in a wood, a clearing.

lang megs *n* a kind of apple.

larick, lairick *n* the larch.

lefter *n* a shallow wooden vessel, larger than a *cog*.

leomen *n* the bough of a tree.

leven *n* an open space between woods.

lifter *n* a shallow, broad wooden bowl, in which milk is put for casting up the cream.

lightin'-in-eldin *n* small brushy fuel, such as furze, thorns, broom, etc.

lind, lynd *n* the lime tree.

lockin'-tree *n* the rung that serves to bar the door.

lompnyt *adj* laid with trees.

lowder *n* a wooden lever; a hand-spoke for lifting a millstone.

luggie, loggie *n* a small wooden vessel, for holding meat or drink, made of staves, one of which projects as a handle, from *lug*, the ear.

luggit or lowgit disch *n* a wooden bowl or vessel with upright handles; an eared dish.

M

match-stick *n* a splint of wood tipped with sulphur, for kindling.

melmont-berry *n* the juniper berry.

mercal *n* a piece of wood used in the construction of the Shetland plough.

met-stick *n* a piece of wood used for taking the measure of a foot.

moss-fa'en *adj* (used of trees) fallen into a bog and gradually covered in moss.

moss-oak *n* bog oak; a seat made of bog-oak.

moss-stock *n* trunks and stumps of bog-oak.

mowdy-brod, mould-board *n* a board on a Scottish plough which turned over the furrow.

mulberry *n* the whitebeam tree.

nacket *n* a bit of wood, stone or bone used in shinty.

nap *n* a little round wooden dish, made of staves; a milk-vat.

nature-wid *n* natural wood.

navus-bore *n* a hole in wood where a knot has dropped out.

neat's-fire, need-fire, neid-fire *n* fire from the friction of two pieces of wood; a beacon-fire; spontaneous combustion, the phosphoric light of rotten wood.

needle *n* a fallen leaf of the larch or Scotch pine; a spark of fire or boiling matter that pricks the spot of skin where it falls.

nirled *adj* (applied to trees) stunted.

nit-wud *n* a wood of hazel-nut trees.

nivlock *n* a bit of wood, around which the end of a hair-tether is fastened.

nurse *n* a hardy tree planted to shelter a more tender one.

nut-brae *n* a *brae* abounding in hazel-nut trees.

nutting-tyne *n* a forked instrument for pulling nuts from the tree.

O

oak-nut *n* an acorn.

ouer-tree *n* the *stilt*, or handle of an Orcadian plough.

oussen-bow *n* a piece of curved wood put round the necks of oxen, as a sort of collar, to which the draught is fixed, now rarely used.

P

pailin, pailing *n* a fence made of stakes.

palissade *n* a row of trees planted close.

palm *n* the common willow; in plural, its catkins.

palmy *adj* abounding in catkins.

pan-wood *n* fuel used at salt-pans for purposes of evaporation.

park *n* a wood, as in "a fir park".

pawmer *n* a palm tree.

pea-tree, pease cod tree *n* the laburnum.

peerie-man *n* an iron or wooden frame for holding bog-wood or *fir-candles* for lighting purposes.

perk-tree *n* a pole to support a clothes-line.

pinler *n* a forester; a field-watcher.

pirn-cap *n* a wooden bowl, used by weavers for holding their quills.

pirn-stick *n* the wooden broach on which the quill is placed when the yarn is reeled off.

plane *n* the sycamore.

plane-tree *n* the maple.

plantin, planting *n* a plantation.

plonk *n* a tree buried in a moss.

plotter-plate *n* a wooden platter with a place in the middle to hold salt.

plump *n* a cluster, this term is evidently used in the same sense with clump, as denoting a tuft of trees or shrubs.

poddock *n* a rude sort of sledge for drawing stones, made of the *glack* of a tree, with narrow pieces of wood nailed across.

pomerie *n* an orchard.

popil *n* a poplar.

poor-page *n* an iron or wooden frame for holding *fir-candles*.

pumpit *adj* hollow; (used of trees) rotten at the core.

pundar *n* a person who has charge of hedges, woods, etc. and who 'pounds' straying cattle.

pye-trees *n* cross-trees or poles for drying nets, yarn.

Q, R

quaking-ash, quaukin-aish *n* the aspen.

quibow *n* a branch of a tree

raaca *n* driftwood.

rabblach *n* a stunted tree.

rack *n* a piece of wood used for the purpose of feeding a mill.

raglat plane *n* a species of plane used by carpenters, in making a groove for shelves of drawers etc.

rammel *n* brushwood; small branches.

rantle, rannle, rantle-tree *n* a wooden or iron bar across a chimney from which a chain and pot hook were suspended.

ran, rantree, rantle-tree, raun, raun-tree, roan-tree *n* the mountain ash, the rowan tree.

rap and stow *phr* a phrase meaning root and branch.

raultree, raeltree *n* a long piece of strong wood placed across byres to put the end of cow-stakes in.

rauntree, rawn-tree *n* the mountain-ash.

red sauch *n* a species of willow.

red-wood *n* the name given to the reddish or dark coloured and more incorruptible wood found at the heart of trees.

reserve *n* a tree reserved in a hag, or the cutting of an allotted portion

RABBLACH

of wood.

rip *v* to cleave; to saw wood with the grain.

rice *n* a twig; a branch; brushwood; branches used for hedging.

rise, rys, rice, ryss *n* a small twig; brushwood; the branches of trees after they are lopped off.

roan *n* a congeries of brushwood.

roden, rodin, roden-tree *n* the mountain ash.

rodden, rudden *n* the berry of the rowan, occasionally the tree itself.

rone, roan, ron *n* a tangle of brushwood, thorns etc.

rosseny *adj* abounding in brushwood.

roughie *n* a withered bough; brushwood; dried heather.

roun, rawn-tree, raun-tree *n* the rowan or mountain ash tree.

rungle-tree, ringil-tree *n* a beam across a chimney or fire for hanging pots on.

runk *n* a broken or twisted and useless branch of a tree.

runt *n* the trunk of a tree; an old decayed tree stump.

ruskie *n* a basket made from twigs and straw for carrying corn.

S

sab, sob *v* to make a hissing sound, as of green wood, etc., in a fire.

sap-spale, sapwood *n* the weak part of wood nearest to the bark.

sauch, sauch-tree, sauchen-tree, saugh *n* various species of the willow, including the goat willow.

sauchen, sauchin, saughin *adj* of or pertaining to willow.

sauchie *adj* abounding with willows.

savorcoll, savorcoil *n* a woodcutter or sawyer; a forester.

sawins *n* sawdust.

scug *n* a twig; a small branch.

schaw *n* a wood of a small size; a glade; a grove.

schawaldouris *n* wanderers in the woods, subsisting by hunting.

schide, schyde, side *n* a billet of wood; a chip; a splinter.

scob *n* a splint; a wooden gag; a limber rod of willow, hazel, etc. used for fastening down thatch.

scoot *n* a wooden drinking cup.

scow *n* a barrel-stave; a thin plank from which barrel-staves are made; the outside board of a tree; a stick; a twig; brushwood, firewood; a bit, fragment; the fragments cut from planks; anything broken in small and useless pieces.

scowb *n* a splint; a sapling.

scrab, scrabble *n* a stunted or withered tree or shrub; a root; a stump of heather; a puny, shrivelled person.

scrabblich *n* a stunted tree or shrub.

screyb *n* the wild apple; the crab apple.

scrog, scrogg *n* a stunted shrub, tree, or branch; a thorn-bush; rough land covered with stunted bushes and underwood, the crab-apple.

scroggie, scroggy *adj* stunted, crooked, thorny, abounding in stunted bushes or underwood.

scrunt, skrunt *n* a stubby branch; a worn out besom.

shank *n* the trunk of a tree.

shaw *n* a wood.

shelter-stell *n* an enclosure or shelter for sheep, of stone or a clump of trees.

siplin, sipplyne *n* a young tree.

sithe-straik *n* a piece of hard wood, pricked and overlaid with grease and flinty sand, used for sharpening a scythe.

skeigh *n* a round, moveable piece of wood, put upon the spindle of the *muckle wheel* used for spinning wool, to prevent the worsted from coming off the spindle.

skelb *n* a splinter of wood.

slae *n* the sloe; the black thorn berry.

slaeie *adj* abounding in sloes or sloe-bushes.

slain, slane *n* a wooden *cleugh* or precipice.

slegger *n* a *janker*; a pole fixed to the axle of two high wheels, used for carrying trees.

smoch *n* the smoke of burning wet, rotten wood.

snag *n, v* a branch broken from a tree; *aik-snag*, the broken bough of an oak; to cut off branches with an axe or bill.

snath, sned, sneth *v* to prune timber-trees; to lop off.

sned *n* a branch pruned off.

snedder *n* a person who prunes.

sneddins, sneddings *n* prunings, or twigs lopped off.

snugs *n* small branches lopped off

a tree.

sooker *n* the sucker of a tree.

spaik *n* a bar of wood; a spoke; a branch or slip of a tree planted to grow; in plural the wooden bars on which a dead body is carried to the grave.

speeock *n* a stake or log of wood.

spelk *n* a splinter; a thin piece of wood.

spelked *adj* (used of wood) ragged.

spire *n* a small tapering tree, generally a fir-tree, of a fit size for paling.

sprot, sprote *n* a small stick or twig often used for fuel, a chip of wood flying from a carpenter's tool, the end of a stalk of grain or a branch of a tree; the end of a stalk of grain, or branch of a tree, blown off by a high wind.

sprush *n* common spruce.

spule *n* a thin, flat piece of wood.

spunk-wood *n* matchwood; small splinters.

square-man *n* a carpenter.

square-wricht *n* a joiner who works in the finer kinds of furniture.

sta'-tree *n* the stake in a cow-house to which a cow is bound.

stake and rice *n* stakes driven into the earth, and thin boughs nailed across.

steel *n* a wooded *cleuch* or precipice, greater than a *slain*.

stoan *v* (used of trees etc.) to send out suckers from the roots, a quantity of suckers from the roots.

stob *n* the stump of a tree.

stog *n* a piece of decayed tree sticking out of the ground.

stool *n* a place where wood springs up spontaneously after having been cut down.

straik *n* a piece of hard wood, with straight edges, used for stroking off all that is above the legal measure of grain, salt etc. in the vessel used for measurement.

strip, stripe *n* a long narrow plantation or belt of trees.

stug, stog *n* a piece of decayed tree standing out of the ground.

stunt *n* a stunted tree.

swee *v* to move backwards and forwards, as a tree, from the action of the wind.

swingle-tree *n* one of the moveable pieces of wood put before a plough or a harrow, to which the traces are fastened.

swirl, swirel *n* a twist in the grain of wood.

swirly *adj* (used of wood) full of twists or knots, contorted, gnarled.

T

tanners *n* the small roots of trees.

tappin, taupin *n* the root of a tree.

tendle, tennel, tennle *n* firewood; brushwood used for fuel.

thivel *n* a cylindrical piece of wood used for stirring pottage etc. in cooking.

thorter *adj* (used of wood) cross grained.

thorter-knot *n* a knot in wood, the *knarry* end of a branch.

timmer *n, adj* timber, wood, beams, rafters; of, or belonging to wood, as *a timmer cap,* a wooden bowl, *a timmer trencher,* a wooden plate.

timmer-breeks *n* a cant term for a coffin.

timmerin *v* a beating with a stick.

timmer-man *n* a carpenter.

tree *n* a tree; a barrel; a staff; an archery bow; a pole or bar of wood; a swingle-tree.

tree-leggit *adj* having a wooden leg.

tree-plate *n* a wooden plate or trencher.

trein, trene, treen *adj* wooden.

trood *n* wood for fences.

trysting-tree *n* a tree at which lovers meet by agreement.

twa-beast-tree *n* the swingle-tree in the Orcadian plough, by which two horses draw.

twist *n* a twig.

twite *v* to whittle wood.

U, V

virideer *n* the keeper of the grass or green wood in a forest.

verger *n* an orchard.

waese, wease *n* a bundle of sticks or brushwood placed on the windward side of a cottage-door to ward off the blast.

wallwood *n* wild-wood.

ware *n* a tough and hard knot in a tree.

warp *v* to make an embankment with piles and brushwood.

warrachie *adj* (as applied to the trunk of a tree) rough and knotty.

warren *adj* of or belonging to the pine tree.

warroch *n* a knotty stick.

wattle *n* a twig, a switch, a billet of wood; a pliant rod, twig or wand.

weedins *n* plants weeded out, or cut out, in thinning trees, turnips, etc.

wheegil *n* a piece of wood for pushing in the end of the straw-rope with which a sheaf is bound.

whirrock *n* a knot in wood caused by the growth of a branch from the place.

whistle-wood *n* a smooth wood used by boys for making whistles; the willow; the plane-tree.

white-legs *n* the smaller wood, branches, etc. of a cutting.

white wood *n* the outermost circles of oak-trees found in peat-bogs.

whitter *n* a tree reserved in cutting timber.

wicker *n* a twig; a wand; a small switch.

wid, widen, widdy *n, adj* wood, wooden, woody.

widdie *n* a twig or wand of willow or tough but flexible wood; a rope made of twigs or willow, used to denote a halter, the term is vulgarly understood as if it denoted the gallows itself; a twig, having several smaller shoots branching out from it; which being plaited together, it is used as a whip, the single grain serving for a handle

cheat the widdie *phr* to escape the gallows, when it has been fully deserved; there is a proverb which every Scotsman has heard, "the water'll no wrang the widdie", conveying the same idea with the adage, "he who is born to be hanged will never be drowned" but expressing the thought alliteratively and poetically.

widdie-nek *n* gallows-neck; one doomed to be hanged.

wiggam-tree *n* the mountain-ash.

willie, willan *n* the willow.

wine-tree *n* the blackthorn.

wiss *n* the moisture exuding from bark in preparing it for tanning.

witches' hazel *n* the mountain ash.

wither-spale *n* a notched piece of wood, whirled round at the end of a string, to mimic thunder.

witter *n* a tree reserved in a general cutting, in what is called a *hag*

wod, wode, woud *n* a wood.

wodfang, wodfaing *n* the right to cut and carry away wood, i.e. firewood, from a forest.

wodhag *n* the annual cutting of wood in a forest.

wod-lynd *n* foliage of the woods; living in the woods, as in "under wod-lynd".

wrack-wid *n* wood cast up by sea.

wright, wricht, wrycht *n* a joiner; the general name for a common carpenter.

wrichtin' *n* the trade of a carpenter.

wud *n* wood.

wuddie-tow *n* a hangman's rope.

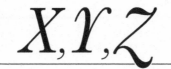

yill-cap, -caup *n* a wooden vessel from which ale is drunk; large, or saucer eyes, as in "yill-caup een".

Part three

Weather

A

airish *adj* chilly.

air-cock *n* weather-cock.

aitrie, aittrie *adj* (applied to the weather) cold, bleak, grim.

airt *n* the quarter of the heavens; point of the compass; the direction of the wind; a direction, way; (used of the wind) to blow from a certain quarter.

aitrie *adj* cold, bleak grim; generally applied to the weather.

allerish *adj* chilly; rather cold, a *snell* morning, as in "allerish morning".

alter *n* a change; a change of weather.

angry teeth *n* the fragment of a rainbow appearing on the horizon, and when seen on the north or east indicating bad weather.

appell *v* to cease to rain.

ark *n* the formation of clouds said to resemble Noah's Ark.

ask *n, v* drizzle; small particles of dust or snow; half-fog half-rain; to rain slightly, to drizzle.

B

Banff-baillies *n* white, snowy-looking clouds on the horizon, betokening foul weather.

baumy *adj* balmy.

beir, bere, bir, bier *n, v* noise, cry, roar; force, impetuosity, often as denoting the violence of the wind.

bensell, bensail, bensil, bent-sail *n* exposure to a violent wind, as in "I am sure ye bade a sair bensel" i.e. suffered a severe attack of the gale; transferred to a place exposed to the violence of a storm and directly opposed to *bield*; "bensil o' the brae", that point of an eminence most exposed to the weather.

birssy *adj* keen, sharp; (applied to weather) a cold, bleak day, as in "a birssy day".

black weather *n* rainy weather.

black-frost *n* frost without rime or snow lying on the round, as opposed to *white* frost, equivalent to hoar frost.

blad *n* a squall; always including the idea of rain; a heavy fall of rain is called "a blad of weet".

bladdy *adj* inconsistent, unsettled, applied to the weather; "a bladdy day" is one alternately fair and foul.

blanch *n* a flash or sudden blaze; as in "a blanch o' lightning".

blash *n* a heavy fall of rain, as in "a blash o' weet".

blashy *adj* rainy, wet, gusty; weak, watery.

blastie *adj* gusty, blustering.

blately *adj* (used of rain) soft, gentle.

blaud *v* to slap; to blow in gusts; to injure.

blaw *v* to blow; in a literal sense, referring to the wind.

blaw *n* a blast, a gust; the direction of the wind; a draught.

blawthir *n* wet weather.

blaze *n* a sudden blast of dry wind.

bleddin' *v* (used of snow-flakes) falling.

bleeze *n* (applied to a dry wind) a sudden blast, as in "a bleeze of wind".

bleffert, bliffert *n* a sudden and violent fall of snow, but not of long continuance; a squall; generally conveying the idea of wind and rain; a storm; a hurricane.

blent up *v* (used of the sun) to shine, after the sky has been overcast.

blenter *n* a boisterous, intermitting wind.

blewder *n* a hurricane.

bliffart *n* a squall.

blind-drift, blin'-drift *n* heavy driving snow; a blinding heavy snow.

blirt *n* a gust of wind, accompanied by rain; a smart, cold shower, with wind; an intermittent drizzle; a cold drift of snow; on the verge of tears.

blirtie *adj* (as applied to the weather) inconstant; "a blirtie day", one that has occasionally severe blasts of wind and rain.

blizzen *adj* drought is said to be *blizzening*, when the wind parches and withers the fruits of the earth.

blout *n* the sudden breaking of a storm; a sudden fall of rain, hail or snow, accompanied with noise, as in "a blout of foul weather".

blouter *n* a blast of wind.

blowy *adj* blowing; gusty.

blue *adj* a very chilly or frosty day,

as in "a blue day".

blue bore *n* a rift or opening in opening in the clouds.

blue-day *n* a day which is bleak and frosty; or a day of uproar or disturbance.

bluffert *v* to bluster, as the wind; the blast sustained in meeting a rough wind or squall.

bluffertin *adj* blustering; gusty.

blyte *n* a blast of bad weather, a flying shower.

boll *n* a flash of lightning.

bomacie *n* (perhaps) thunder; a thunderstorm.

bor, b *n* an opening in the clouds when the sky is thick and gloomy, or during rain, is called a "blue bore".

borie *n* a clear opening in the sky in wet weather.

borrowing days *n* the last three days of March, old style. These days being generally stormy, our forefathers have endeavoured to account for this circumstance by pretending that March borrowed them from April that he might extend his power so much longer. Those who are much addicted to superstition will neither borrow nor lend on any of these days, lest the articles borrowed should be employed for the purposes of witchcraft against the lenders.

boulder, bowder *n* a great squall; a strong blast of wind.

boule *n* a clear opening in the clouds in a dark, rainy day, prognosticating fair weather.

bowt *n* a thunderbolt.

brack *n* a quantity of snow or earth shooting from a hill; a flood, when the ice *breaks* in consequence of a thaw; a sudden and heavy fall of rain.

brak *v* breaking up, as in "the brak of a storm".

brashy, braushie *adj* stormy.

break down *v* (used of the weather) to become wet or stormy.

breek *v* (used by females shearing on a rainy day) tucking up their petticoats to their knees, in form of breeches. The question is often asked, "are ye gaun to breek the day?".

brim *adj* bleak; exposed to the weather.

broch, bough, brugh *n* (applied to the moon) the hazy ring or ruff which surrounds the moon in certain states of the atmosphere. Its appearance is said to indicate a coming storm of rain or snow.

bruckly *adj* brittle; (used of the weather) uncertain, changeable.

bub *n* a blast; a gust of severe weather.

buff *n* a puff or blast of wind.

C

cairie *n, v* the motion of clouds in stormy weather.

calledin-o'-the-blade *n* a slight shower which cools and refreshes grass.

carmudgelt *adj* made soft by lightning.

carry *n* a term used to express the motion of the clouds before the wind; improperly used for the firmament or sky.

cast up *v* (applied to clouds) when they rise from the horizon, so as to threaten rain.

castin' up *phr* the sky is beginning to clear, after rain or very louring weather.

cat-hair, cat's-hair *n* names given to the streaky streaming clouds called *cirrus* and *cirro-stratus*.

cauts *n* the tremulous appearance near the surface of the ground in hot sunshine. *See also* king's weather.

cavaburd *n* a thick fall of snow.

caver *n* a gentle breeze moving the water slightly.

chill-cauld *adj* nearly frozen.

cock's-eye *n* a halo that appears round the moon and indicates stormy weather.

cow-craik *n* a mist with an easterly wind, as in "the cow-craik destroys a' the fruit".

clood *n* cloud.

crancreugh, cranreuch, cran-reuth, craundroch *n* hoar frost; rime.

cranrochie *adj* abounding with hoar-frost.

crisp *v* to crackle, as ground under the feet in a slight frost.

cum *on v* to rain; it's beginning to rain, as in "it's cumin on".

D

dacklin *n* a slight shower, as in "a dacklin of rain".

dag, dagg *v, n* to rain gently; a thick or drizzling rain; a thick fog; a mist; a heavy shower, dew.

daggered *adj* (used of lightning) forked.

daggie *adj* drizzling; a day characterised with light rain, as in "a daggie day".

daggle *v* to fall in torrents.

dahie *adj* (used of weather) warm, misty, muggy.

darden *n* a dry, soft wind.

dasie, daizie *adj* (used of the weather) cold, damp raw, sunless, chilling.

dash *n* a sudden fall of rain.

dawch *v* to moisten, as with dew.

dawghie, dawkie, dawky, dauky *adj* moist, a day characterized by thick mist, or by drizzling rain, as in "a dawkie day".

dawk *n, v* a drizzling rain; to drizzle.

daugh *n* a very heavy dew, or drizzling rain.

dead-lown *adj* completely still; (applied to the atmosphere) a dead calm.

deasie *adj* (used of the weather) cold, raw, uncomfortable.

deaw *v* to rain gently, to drizzle.

deid-day *n* a calm, dull, winter day.

dish *v* to rain heavily.

dissle *v* to drizzle.

dissle *n* a slight shower, a slight wetness on standing corn, the effect of a *drizzling* rain.

docken, doken *n* the dock, a herb; a stormy day, at whatever season of the year, sometimes a day distinguished by a quarrel, as in "a day amang the dockens".

doggindales *n* clouds of mist clinging to hill-sides, betokening southerly winds.

doister *n* a storm from the sea; a hurricane; a strong, steady breeze.

doon-come, doon-lay *n* a heavy fall of rain, snow, sleet.

doun-ding *n* sleet or snow.

dowden *v* to toss about with the wind.

down-ding *n* a very heavy fall of

rain.

down-pour *n* an excessively heavy fall of rain.

dreel *n* a swift, violent motion; a hurricane, as in "a dreel o' wind"; blowing weather.

dreepie *adj* (used of the weather) dripping, wet.

driffle *n* a drizzling rain.

driffle *v* to drizzle.

drifling *n* a small rain.

drift *n* flying snow, especially including the idea of its being forcibly driven by the wind; a drove of cattle etc.; a flock of birds, snow etc. driven by wind.

drifty *adj* abounding with snow-drift; a gusty snowy day, as in "a drifty day".

droppy *adj* (used of occasional and seasonal showers) as in "it's droppy weather".

drouth *n* drought.

drow *n* a squall; a severe gust; a cold mist approaching to rain.

drowie, *adj* moist; misty, as in "a drowie day".

drucht *n* drought, a season of drought.

druchty *n* dry weather.

E

eard-din *n* thunder; thunder in the earth; an earthquake.

emmis *adj* variable; (used of the weather) gloomy.

erd-drift, erdrift *n* a snow or hail driven violently by the wind from off the earth; opposed to *yowden-drift*, which signifies snow or hail blown directly and forcibly from the heavens.

eterie, etrie *adj* keen, bitter; (applied to the weather) as in "an etrie sky"; also ill-humoured, ill-tempered.

evendoun *adj* denoting a very heavy fall of rain.

ewden-drift, ewindrift *n* snow drifted by the wind.

F

faggie *adj* fatiguing, as in "a faggie day", one that tires or *fags* one by its sultriness.

fair *adj, v* calm; (used of the weather) to become fine, to clear up; (applied to the atmosphere) preceding rain.

fairding *v* violent blowing.

fat-a-feck *adj* (used of the weather) favourable, seasonable.

faul *n* a halo round the moon, indicating a fall of rain.

feeding storm *n* a fall of snow, which is on the increase, and threatens to lie deep on the ground.

fern-storm *n* rain caused by the burning of fern or heather.

feuchter *n* a slight fall of snow.

filly-tails *n* fleecy cirrus clouds.

fire *v* (applied to grass, grain or foliage) to scorch by hot winds or lightning;

fire-levin, -flaucht, -saucht *n* lightning.

fissle *v* to make a rustling noise, as the wind when it shakes the leaves of trees.

flachten *n* a flake of snow.

flag *n* a squall; a flash of lightning; a flake of snow.

flagartie *adj* squally, snowy.

flaght, flacht *n* a flash of lightning, as in "a flaght o' fire".

flam *n* a sudden puff of wind.

flan *n, adj, v* a gust of wind; shallow, flat; to come in gusts, as in "the wind's flannin down the lum".

flaurie *n* a drizzle.

flaw *n* a blast of wind; a storm of snow.

flechin, flichen, flichan, flighen, flichter *n* a flake of snow.

fleckit *adj* (used of the sky) dappled with clouds.

fleechin *adj* (applied to the weather) falsely assuming a favourable appearance; as in "that's a fleechin day", i.e. a day that promises much more than will be performed.

flist *n* a squall; a flying shower of snow.

flistin *n* a slight shower.

flisty *adj* stormy, squally.

flobby *adj* (used of clouds) large and heavy indicating rain.

floichen *n* an uncommonly large flake of snow.

flouncing *v* (used of trees in a gale) tossing to and fro.

flup *n* sleet.

folm *n* (used of the weather) a long spell, of mist etc.; a volume of rolling cloud.

forcing *adj* (used of the weather) likely to bring crops to maturity.

foul *adj* (used of the weather) bad, gloomy.

fresh *adj* (used of the weather) thawing, wet, cold, open.

frog *n, v* a flying shower of snow or sleet; to snow or sleet at intervals.

frost *v* to injure by frost, as in "the potatoes are a' frostit"; to become frost-bitten.

fudder *n* a gust of wind; a flurry; the shock, impulse or resistance, occasioned by a blistering wind.

fudder-flash *n* a flash of lightning.

fuddum *n* snow drifting at intervals.

fyoonach *n* (used of snow) a sprinkle, as much as just whitens the ground.

G

gall winde *n* a gale.

gast *n* a gust of wind.

gell *adj* (used of the weather) sharp; keen.

girslin *n* a slight frost; a thin scuff of ice.

give *v* to yield, to give way, as in "the frost gives", a phrase expressive of a change in the morning from frost to open weather.

glaff *n* a sudden blast; as in "a glaff o' wind".

glaister *n* a thin covering; as of snow or ice, as in "there's a glaister o' ice the day".

glaisterie *adj* "a glaisterie day", one on which snow falls and melts.

glashtroch *adj* a term expressive of continued rain, and the concomitant dirtiness of the roads.

gloff *n* a sudden, partial, and transitory change of the atmosphere surrounding a person, caused by a change in the undulation; the sensation produced by this change, as in "I fand a great gloff o' heat";

it is also applied to darkness, when occasionally it appears denser to the eye than in other parts of the atmosphere.

gloggie *adj* (applied to the atmosphere) dark and hazy, misty.

glottenin *n* a partial thaw.

glousterie *adj* boisterous. The phrase "a glousterin day", denotes that unequal state of the weather, in consequence of which it sometimes rains, and at other times blows; in some places it is applied to a day in which there is rain accompanied with a pretty strong wind. When there is some appearance of a fall of snow, the term *gloushterioch* is applied to the weather.

gloweret-like *adj* stormy looking.

glouf, gluff *n* a sudden blast.

glouten *v, n* to thaw gently; a partial thaw.

glushie *adj* abounding with snow in a state of liquification, as in "the road's awfu' glushie".

gludder *n* the sound caused by a body falling among mire.

gnaw *n* a slight, partial thaw.

Gonial-blast *n* a great storm in January 1794, in the south of Scotland, destroying many sheep.

goor *n, adj* broken ice and half-melted snow in a thaw; (used of streams) to become choked with masses of ice and snow in a thaw.

gouling *adj* a term applied to stormy weather; one marked by strong wind, as in "a gouling day".

gouster *v* to storm with wind or rain.

gousterous-looking *adj* stormy-looking.

gousty *adj* tempestuous; stormy; gusty.

goutte *n* a drop; a large drop of rain.

gow *n* a halo; a cloudy, colourless circle surrounding the disc of the sun or moon.

gowan-gabbit *adj* (used of the sky) bright, fine, deceptively clear.

gowk-storm, gowk's storm *n* a storm consisting of several days of tempestuous weather, believed by the peasantry periodically to take place about the beginning of April, at the time that the *gowk*, or cuckoo, visits the country.

gowling *adj* boisterous; stormy.

grashloch *adj* stormy; boisterous, a windy, blustery day, as in "a grash-loch day".

grey, gray *n* "grey o' the morning", dawn of the day; a slight breath of wind.

grow weather *adj* (applied to the weather) favourable to vegetable growth.

grue *v* to sigh or groan like wind

before a storm.

gull *n* chill; a thin, cold mist, accompanied by a slight wind, as in "a cauld gull nicht."

gurly *adj* (applied to the weather) boisterous, threatening to be stormy, bitter.

H

haar *n* a fog; a chilly, foggy, easterly wind.

haar-clouds *n* clouds brought by a raw, cold wind from the east.

haary *adj* (used of wind) cold, keen, biting.

hagger *n* a small rain; it rains gently, as in "it's haggerin".

hail *v* to pour down.

hair-frost *n* hoar frost.

hale water *n* a phrase denoting a very heavy fall of rain, in which it comes down as if poured out of buckets.

handsome *adj* (used of the weather) fine, bright.

hap *n* a heavy fall or cover of snow.

harr *n* a breeze from the east.

haud *n* a squall; a whirlwind.

haugull *n* a cold and damp easterly wind blowing from the sea in summer.

haugullin' *adj* (applied to the weather) drizzling, damp and cold; marked by a good deal of drizzling, as in "a haugullin' day".

haur *n* a cold, easterly wind, bringing fog.

hearkenin'-win' *n* a comparative lull in a storm, followed by a destructive blast.

heavy-heartit *adj* (used of the atmosphere) lowering, threatening rain.

helm of weet *n* a great fall of rain.

henscarts *n* fleecy clouds thought to betoken wind or rain.

howder *n* a strong blast of wind.

hullerie *adj* (applied to the state of the atmosphere) raw, damp and cold, as in "that's a hullerie day".

hurloch, urloch *adj* cloudy.

hurly-burly *n, v* a storm of wind; tempestuous, tumultuous.

huther *n, v* a wetting mist; raining slightly, as in "it's hutherin'".

I

ill *adj* stormy.

immis *adj* (used of the weather) variable; foggy.

indumious *adj* very bad; (used of the weather) extraordinarily stormy.

insook *n* (used of frost) a touch, a slight amount; (used of the tide) an inrush.

istick *n* a slight temporary frost.

it's drowin' on *phr* used to denote a thick wetting mist.

J

jabbled *adj* stormy.

jock-startle-a-stobie *n* exhalations from the ground on a warm summer day.

jock-te-leear *n* a vulgar cant term for a small almanac, from its loose prognostications with regard to the weather.

jorum *n* a loud thunder-crash.

K

kevel *n* a gentle breeze, causing a slight motion of the water.

king's weather *n* the exhalations arising from the earth on a warm day.

kittle *v* (used of the wind) when it rises; beginning to rise, as in "it's beginning to kittle".

L

laikin, laiky *adj* (used of rain) intermittent.

Lammas flude, Lammas spate *n* the heavy fall of rain which generally takes place sometime in the month of August, causing a swell in the waters.

land-burst *n* a series of a few breakers at a tidal change, or occasionally during a storm.

landlash *n* a great fall of rain, accompanied with high wind.

lash *n* a heavy fall or rain; it rains heavily, as in "it's lashin' on".

laughing-rain *n* rain from the south-west, with a clear sky line.

lay *v* (used of crops) to flatten by wind or rain.

lay on *v* to rain, to hail, to snow heavily.

le, lee, lie, lye *n* shelter; security from the tempest.

leesh, leish, leitch *n* a heavy fall of rain.

leisome *adj* warm; sultry.

leper-dew *n* a cold frosty dew.

leven *n* lightning.

levin-bolt *n* a thunder-bolt.

lichtening *n* dawn; daybreak; lightning.

Liddisdale drow *n* a shower that wets an Englishman to the skin.

lift-fire *n* lightning.

lither *adj,* a yielding sky, when the clouds undulate, as in "a lither sky".

loomy *adj* misty; hazy.

lounlie, lownly *adj, v* screened from the wind, as in "we'll stand braw and lownly ahint the wa'".

loury *adj* (used of the weather) gloomy, threatening.

lowden *adj, v* (used of the wind) to signify that it has fallen.

lown *adj, v* calm; serene; sheltered; (used of the wind) to abate, fall.

lum *v* to rain heavily.

lumming *adj* a term applied to the weather when there is thick rain.

lunkie *adj* sultry, denoting the oppressive state of the atmosphere before rain or thunder.

lunkieness *n* oppressiveness of atmosphere.

lying–storm *n* a prolonged storm.

lythe *v, adj* to shelter; sheltered from the weather.

M

mak up for *v* (used of rain) to threaten.

mask *v* (used of a storm) to be brewing.

mare's-tails *n* long, streaky clouds portending rain.

May-gobs *n* cold weather about the second week in May.

merciful *adj* (used of the weather) favourable, seasonal, mild.

milldew *n* cold, raw weather; wet, foggy weather.

milt-token *n* prognosticating weather from cuts in the spleen of an ox killed about Martinmas.

mist fawn *n* mist like a white spot of ground.

moorawav *n* a thick shower of snow.

mooth *adj* foggy, misty; drizzling weather.

moth *adj* warm, sultry.

mug *v* to drizzle.

mug, muggle *n* a drizzling rain.

muggly *adj* drizzling; damp, foggy.

muith *adj* (applied to the weather) warm and misty; foggy, damp and warm.

nizzlin *n* direct exposure to a severe storm.

Noah's ark *n* clouds assuming the shape of a boat, regarded as a sign of the weather.

noof *adj* sheltered from the weather.

nooh, nough, now *v* (used of the wind) to blow gently.

nor-wastert *n* a bitter blast; anything of a cold, rude, nature.

nose-feast *n* a storm.

nose-nippin' *adj* (used of the weather) cold, freezing; *snell.*

nyatter *v* to rain slightly with a high wind.

O

o'erblaw *v* (used of a storm) to blow over; to cover with driven snow.

o'ergaffin *adj* clouded; overcast.

o'ercast *v, adj* to cloud over, to overcast.

onding *n* a fall of rain or snow, but especially the latter.

ondingin *n* rain or snow; as in "there'll be a heap o' ondingin".

onfall *n* a fall of rain or snow.

onfeel *adj* unpleasant, disagreeable, as in "an onfeel day".

open *adj* (used of the weather) mild, without frost or snow.

oncome, onlay *n* a fall of rain or snow.

ouchin' *v* (used of the wind) sighing, blowing gently.

ouder, owder *n* a light mist or haze, such as is sometimes seen at sun-rise; the flickering exhalations from the ground, in the sunshine of a warm day.

ouergaff *v* (applied to the sky) when it begins to be clouded; to overcast.

ough *v* (used of the wind) to blow gently.

outerly *adv* outwards; (used of the wind) blowing from the shore.

outpour *n* a downpour of rain or snow.

P

packies *n* heavy masses of clouds.

pappin *v* a thrashing; the sound made by hail.

peeggirin-blast *n* a stormy blast; a heavy shower.

peel-a-bane *n* very freezing weather.

peengie, peenjie *adj* not able to endure cold.

pet *adj* a term applied to a good day when the weather is generally bad.

peuchling *n* a slight fall of snow.

pewil, pewl, peughle *v* used to denote the falling of snow in small particles, without continuation, during a severe frost.

pine *v* (used of wind) to blow strongly.

piner *n* a strong breeze from the North or North East.

pir, per *n* a breeze, a flaw of wind.

pirl *v* to be gently rippled, as the surface of water by a light wind.

plash *n* a heavy fall of rain.

plump *n, v* a heavy shower falling straight down; to rain heavily.

plype *n* a heavy rain; a fall into water.

puft *n* a puff of wind.

Q

quail *v* (used of the wind) to lull, to quiet down.

R

rack up *v* when the clouds begin to open, so that the sky is seen.

racky *adj* (used of the weather) gusty, stormy.

raff *n* a flying shower.

ragglish, raglish *adj* (used of the weather) rough, boisterous.

rak *n* a thick mist or fog.

rake *n* a swift pace; the direction of clouds driven by the wind; a journey.

raking *v* (used of clouds) gathering, scouring.

ralliach *adj* slightly stormy.

rambaleugh *adj* tempestuous, a stormy day. as in "a rambaleugh day".

rasch *v, n* to pour down; a heavy fall of rain, as in "a raschin rain".

rauky, rawky *adj* misty, foggy; the same as *rooky*; foggy, damp, raw and cold.

rave *v* (used of the wind) to make a wild, roaring sound.

raw *adj* (used of the weather) cold and damp.

rawk *n* a mist, fog.

rawlie *adj* moist; damp; raw; when the air is moist, as in "a rawlie day".

rawn *n* the fragment of a rainbow.

reaving-wind *n* a high wind.

ree *n* a continuation of stormy weather.

reemish, reemie *n* the sound of a heavy fall of snow.

reese *n* "a reese o' wind", a high wind, a stiff breeze.

reesin, reezin *adj* vehement; strong; forcible; a strong, dry, wind, as in "a reezin wind".

ridiculous *adj* (used of the weather) unseasonable.

rime *n* fog; mist; the death-sweat.

rind, rynd, rine, rhynd *n* hoar frost.

ripple *v* to drizzle; (applied to the atmosphere) "the clouds are rippling", they are beginning to sep-arate, so as to indicate a cessation of rain.

rive *v* (used of clouds) to break; (used of a storm) to rage.

riving *adj* energetic; (used of a storm) raging.

roak *n* mist, vapour, fog.

roaky *adj* damp, foggy, misty.

roik, rook *n* a thick mist.

rok *n* (perhaps) a storm.

roos *n* a fine rain accompanied by high wind.

roupy-weather *n* foggy weather that makes one hoarse.

routing-well *n* a well that makes a rumbling sound, predicting a storm.

rumballiach *adj* (applied to the weather) stormy.

S

sab *n* a gust, a gale of wind; a land-storm.

saft *adj* (used of the weather) damp, drizzling, rainy.

Saint Causlan's flaw *n* a shower of snow in March.

sair *adj* (used of the weather) tempestuous.

sapless *adj* (used of the weather) rainless, dry.

sappy *adj* saturated with moisture: sodden; wet; rainy; muddy.

sawr *n* a gentle breeze.

scaffie, scaffy *n* a smart but transient shower; showers which soon blow by, as in "scaffie showers"; a pretty severe shower, as in "a caul' scaff o' a shower".

scarrow *v* to emit a faint light; to shine through clouds; it is said of the moon, "it is scarrowing".

scaumy *adj* misty, hazy.

schore *n* a shower.

scoor, scour *n* the rattle of a hail-shower; a shower; a squall of rain.

scoury, scowrie *adj* showery; squally; a flying shower, as in "a scowrie shower".

scouther, scowther *n* a flying shower.

scouthered *adj* spoiled by rain.

scoutherie *adj* abounding with flying showers; threatening such showers, as in "scoutherie-like".

scoutherin *n* a slight quantity of fallen snow.

scowr *n* a slight shower; a passing summer shower.

scroch *v* (used of a sultry oppressive day, or a withering wind) to scorch.

scrow *n* a slight shower of rain.

scuddrie *adj* showery.

scuff *n* a sudden and passing shower of rain; a puff of wind.

scull-gab *n* a cloud shaped like a boat.

sea-dog *n* a meteor seen on the horizon before sunrise or after sunset, viewed by sailors as a sure portent of bad weather.

sea-haa *n* a sea fog.

sea-hack *n* a temporary thaw occasioned by the salt vapour during the rising tide; a short thaw between frosts.

seugh *n, v* a hollow murmuring sound, a gushing sound like that of the wind.

shak-wind *n* a wind that shakes the ripened grain; a blustering wind.

sheet *v* to fall at brief intervals of sunshine.

shellachie *adj* (used of the weather) cold, piercing.

shilly *adj* (used of the wind) shrill, howling, loud.

shoggle *n* an icicle.

showerickie, showerockie *n* a slight or gentle shower.

shug *n* mist; fog.

sift *v* (used of snow) to fall in fine flakes as through a sieve.

sitten-doun *adj* (used of the weather) settled.

skail *n* a hurricane; a scattering wind or storm.

skail-wind *n* a hurricane.

skalve *n* snow on broad flakes.

skarrach *n* a flying shower; a blast of wind and rain.

skeetlie *n* a drop; a small shower.

skeldroch *n* hoar-frost.

skenydoager, skeyndouger *n* a slight peal of thunder.

skiffer *v* to rain, snow or hail slightly.

skift, skifter *n* a flying shower.

skimmer *v* (used of light) to flicker; to shimmer; to fall in a light drizzling shower.

skour, skowther, skrow *n* a slight shower.

skub *n* a thick fog.

sky *v* (perhaps) to skim along the horizon; "to sky up", to clear up, a phrase used concerning the atmosphere, when the rain seems to go off; "it's skying", the sky is appearing.

skyte *n* a flying shower.

skytie *n* a small, transient shower.

sleek *n* snow and rain mixed; sleet.

slevery *adj* (used of the weather) damp, wet.

slew-fire *n* a designation for lightning.

slounge *n* a great fall of rain.

slud *n* the interval between squally showers.

smir *n* fine rain.

smirn *v* to drizzle.

smolt, smout *adj* (applied to the weather) clear, mild.

smoor *n* a drizzling mist or rain.

smoorich *n* a cloud of dust, smoke, or driving snow, likely to choke one.

smoor-thow *n* heavy snow with strong wind, threatening to suffocate one.

smorie *adj* "a smorie day", a day distinguished by close small rain without wind, a close atmosphere.

smore thow *n* a heavy snow, accompanied by a strong wind, which, as it were, threatens to *smore*, or smother one.

smuggy *adj* muggy; foggy; drizzling.

smurack, smuragh *n* a slight summer shower; a slight drizzle.

smurr *n* a drizzling rain; a fine rain; snow falling thickly.

smush, smushle *n* a light drizzling rain.

sniauve, snyaave, snyauve *v* to snow.

snaw-brack *n* a thaw.

snaw-powther *n* fine snow.

snaw-tooried *adj* snow capped.

snaw-wreathed *adj* blocked by snow-drifts.

snawie, snayaavie, snyaavie *adj* snowy.

sneety *adj* sleety.

snelly *adj* (applied to the weather) keenly.

snifterin' *n* a severe exposure to stormy weather.

snip, sneep *v* the dazzling of something white, as of snow.

snippin *adj* dazzling, as in "the snippin snow".

snouthie *adj* drizzly, dark and rainy; snowy.

sob *n* a land storm; a gust of wind.

soft *adj* wet, rainy; as in "a soft day".

soften *v* to thaw.

sooch, soogh *n, v* a hollow, murmuring sound; the sighing of the wind.

spate *n* a flood; a sudden flood in the river sudden heavy downfall of rain.

speen-drift, spindrift *n* the snow when drifted from the ground by the wind.

spit *v* to rain slightly.

spitter *n, v* a very slight shower; snow, in small particles, driven by the wind; a few drops of rain are falling, as in "it's spitterin".

spleutterie *adj* (used of the weather) very rainy.

spluttery *adj* weak and watery; rainy.

spune-drift *n* snow drifted from the ground by a whirling wind.

squeever *n* a squall of wind.

squib *n* (used of lightning) a flash.

starrach *adj* (used of the weather) cold, disagreeable, boisterous.

startle *v* to run wildly about, as cows do in hot weather.

startle-o'-stovie *n* undulating exhalations seen rising from the ground in very hot weather.

steepin' *v* a drenching with rain.

stew *v* to rain slightly; to drizzle; a rain so thin it resembles a vapour; used like *stour*, to denote spray.

stivven *n, v* freezing weather; to stiffen with cold.

stob *n* that part of a rainbow which seems to rest on the horizon when no more of it is seen.

stock-storm *n* snow continuing to lie on the ground.

stoor *n* a stiff breeze.

storm *n* a fall of snow; *a feeding-storm*, fall after fall of snow, without dissolving.

storm-stead, storm-staid *v, adj* stopped or stayed, in a journey, by reason of a storm.

storming *n* tempestuous weather.

stove *n* a vapour; a ground mist.

stump *n* a fragment of a rainbow appearing on the horizon.

summer-blink *n* a transient gleam of sunshine.

summer-cloks *n* sunbeams dancing in the atmosphere of a fine summer day.

summer-couts *n* the exhalations seen to ascend from the ground in a warm day; the gnats which dance in clusters on a summer evening.

summer-haar *n* a slight breeze from the east, which rises after the sun has passed the meridian.

summer-sob *n* a summer storm; frequent slight rains in summer.

sump *n, v* a sudden and heavy fall of rain; to be wet; to soak, to drench.

sunsheeny *adj* bright with sunshine.

sunways *adv* with the sun, from east to west.

sun-broch *n* a sunbeam; a gleam of sunshine.

sun-glaff *n* a passing sunbeam.

surly *adj* stormy.

sush, sushin *n, v* (used of the wind) a rushing sound.

swack *n* a gust; a severe blast.

swaf *n* a gust, a blast, a swirl of wind.

swathe *n* a wreathe of mist.

swayed *v* (used of growing grass etc.) waved by the wind.

swechynge *n, v* a hollow whistling sound, as of that made by the wind.

swiff *n, v* a term used to denote the hollow melancholy sound made by the wind.

swivvle *n* a strong current of wind sweeping round a corner.

T

tahie *adj* (used of the weather) warm and moist.

taissle *v* applied to the action of the wind when boisterous, as in "I was sair taisslit wi' the wind".

tangle, tankle *n* an icicle.

teem *v* to rain heavily.

teeth *n* the fragment of a rainbow appearing on the horizon, when seen in the north or east, viewed as indicating bad weather.

teuchit-storm *n* the gale, in the reckoning of the vulgar, conjoined with the arrival of the green plover.

thickness *n* fog, mist.

thow *v* to thaw.

thow-hole *n* a name for the south, as, the wind generally blows out of this quarter in the time of a thaw.

thow-lousin *n* a thaw.

thow-wind *n* a wind bringing a thaw.

thuddering *v* (used of the wind) blowing in gusts.

thunder-plump, -speat, -spate *n* a heavy thunder shower.

thwankin' *adj* (applied to clouds) mingling in thick and gloomy succession.

tiff *n* a sudden gust of wind.

tiffle *n* a slight breeze or ripple of wind.

tiordin *n* thunder.

tirl *v* (applied to the wind) to change; to veer about.

tirl-o'-win *n* a good winnowing wind.

tittersome *adj* (used of the weather) fickle, unsettled.

toom o' rain *n* a heavy torrent of rain.

tourbillon *n* a whirlwind.

touttie *adj* throwing into disorder; windy, as in "a touttie wind".

tow-lowsing *n* a thaw.

trash o' weet *n* a heavy fall of rain.

trashie *adj* rainy, as in "trashie weather".

tume *n* "a tume of rain", a sudden and heavy fall of rain.

tuquheit storm *n* a designation given to the storm which almost invariably occurs in the month of March, and which is conjoined, in the traditional observations of the peasantry, with the reappearance of the lapwing from its retreat during the winter.

TOOM O' RAIN

U

unfothersum, unfurthersome *adj* (used of the weather) not favourable to vegetation.

unhearty *adj* uncomfortable; (applied to the state of the atmosphere) a day that is cold and damp, as in "an unhearty day".

upcasting *v* the rising of clouds above the horizon, especially as threatening rain.

upgang *n* (often applied to the weather) a sudden increase of wind and sea.

uppil *adj, v* (used of the weather) clear, clearing up, when the weather at any time has been wet and ceases to be so, we say it is *uppled*.

uppil aboon *adj, n* clear overhead; dry weather.

upright, uplicht *n* brightening after a shower.

upshlag *n* a thaw.

upslay *v* a breaking up of fine weather.

urlich, urluch *adj* cloudy, dull.

V, W

vicious *adj* (of the weather) severe.

wachie *adj* wet; foggy; swampy.

wackness *n* humidity.

wadder *n* weather.

wak *adj, n* moist; watery; rainy; a rainy day, as in "a wak day"; damp, the moistness of the atmosphere.

waknes *n* humidity.

waterfast *adj* capable of resisting

the force of rain.

water-gaw *n* the fragment of a rainbow appearing in the horizon; seen in the north or east, a sign of bad weather.

waufle *n* a slight fall of snow.

waufle *adj* to waver in the air, as snow, chaff, or any light substance.

weather *n* a fall of rain or snow, accompanied with boisterous wind;

a storm; rough weather.

weather-brack *n* a break or change in the weather.

weather-dame *n* weather-prophetess.

weather-days *n* the time for sheep-shearing.

weather-fu' *adj* boisterous, stormy.

weather-gaw *n* part of one side of a rainbow; any change in the atmosphere, known from experience to presage bad weather; any day too good for the season, indicating that it will be succeeded by bad weather.

weather-gleam, weddie-glim, weddir-glim *n* clear sky near the horizon; spoken of objects seen in the twilight or dusk; "between him and the weddir-glim", between him and the light of the sky.

weather-wear *n* the severity or wearing influence of the weather.

weather-wiseacre *n* a weather-prophet; one who is weather-wise.

weathery, weatherie *adj* stormy.

weet, weit *adj, v* wet; to rain; the rain is about to fall, as in "it's ga'in to weet".

weety *adj* rainy; wet, as in "a weety day".

weetness *n* wet, rainy weather.

wheerny *n* a very gentle breeze.

whicker o' a shower *n* a sharp shower, conveying the idea of the noise made by it on a window.

whidder *n, v* a gust of wind; (used of the wind) to bluster.

whiddy *adj* (used of the wind) unsteady, one that shifts about, as in "a whiddy wind".

white shower *n* a shower of snow.

whudder *v* to make a whizzing or rushing sort of noise; the wind in a cold night is said to *whudder.*

wicker *adj* "wicker o' a shower", a short sharp shower.

widder-gaw *n* an abnormally fine day, sometimes portending bad weather to follow.

wild-like *adj* (used of weather) threatening storm.

wind-feed *n* occasional showers which increase the force of the wind.

wind-flaucht *adj* with impetuous motion, as driven by the wind.

windle *v* to walk wearily in the wind.

windy Saturday *n* a peculiarly windy day, which like *black-* or *mirk-Monday* became a traditional era from which subsequent events were dated.

winny *adj* windy.

wither-gloom *n* the clear sky near the horizon.

wrede *n* a snowdrift.

X, Y, Z

yield *n* the influence of the sun on frost.

yird-drift, yowden-drift *n* snow lifted up from the ground, and driven by the wind.

yirdin *n* thunder; an earthquake.

youder *n* a haze; flickering ground exhalations in heat.

Part four

Birds

A

ailsa-cock, ailsa-parrot *n* the puffin.

air-goat *n* the snipe.

aiten *n* the partridge; (perhaps) *ait-hen*, a fowl that feeds among the oats.

aith-hennes *n* (perhaps) heath hens, having been bred on the heath.

alamonti *n* the storm finch, a fowl.

allanhawk *n* the great northern diver; Richardson's skua.

ammer-goose *n* the great northern diver or ember-goose.

arran-ake *n* the speckled diver.

arrondell *n* the swallow.

arseEne *n* the quail.

assilag *n* the stormy petrel.

atteille, atteal, attile *n* (perhaps) the wigeon; being distinguished from the teal.

attile, attile-duck *n* a waterfowl, also called the pochard or poker.

awp, whaup *n* the curlew.

awteal *n* a small teal, not much larger than a snipe.

B

badoch *n* a marine bird of a black colour.

badock *n* the common skua; the arctic gull.

bakie *n* the black-headed gull.

bairdie *n* the whitethroat.

baivie *n* (applied to a numerous family, to a covey of partridges etc.) a large collection.

basket-hinger *n* the gold-crested wren.

basser-goose, bass-goose *n* the gannet.

baukie *n* the razorbill or auk.

bawgie *n* the great black and white gull.

beagle *n* a duck.

bear-buntling *n* a bird like a thrush, haunting especially growing bear.

bear-seed-bird *n* the yellow wagtail.

beck *v* the call of the grouse.

beer-buntlin, beer-bunting *n* the corn bunting.

beld cyttis, bell kytis *n* bald kites; (perhaps) the bald buzzard or marsh harrier.

bell-ringer *n* the long-tailed titmouse.

beltie *n* a water-hen.

beuter, bewter *n* the bittern.

bick and birr *v* to cry as grouse.

big *v* to build a nest.

big mavis *n* the mistle thrush.

big-ox-eye *n* the great titmouse.

billy, billy-whitethroat *n* the golden warbler.

bir *v* a cry or whizzing sound made by birds.

birbeck *n* the call of the moorcock or grouse.

birring *v* the noise made by partridges when they spring.

birrit, birritie *n* the hedge sparrow; the willow warbler.

bissarte, bissette, bizzard *n* the buzzard; a kind of hawk.

black-cap *n* the coal-tit.

black-cock *n* the heath-cock, black game.

black-dooker *n* the cormorant.

black-headed tomtit *n* the great tit.

black hudie *n* the coal-head; the black-headed bunting.

black martin *n* the swift.

blacknebbit crow *n* the carrion crow.

black ox-eye *n* the coal titmouse.

blakwak *n* the bittern.

bleater, blitter *n* the cock snipe, so named from its bleating sound.

blind dorbie *n* the purple sand-piper.

blue sleeves *n* the hen harrier.

blue sparrow *n* the hedge-sparrow.

blue Tom *n* the hedge-sparrow.

blue yaup *n* the fieldfare.

blue-bannet *n* the blue titmouse.

blue-bonnet *n* the blue-cap, or titmouse.

blue-gled *n* the hen harrier.

blue-hawk *n* the sparrow-hawk.

bob-robin *n* the robin.

bobby *n* the robin; the devil.

bog-bluter, bog-bumper *n* the bittern.

bog-gled *n* the moor buzzard.

bonnetie *n* the little grebe.

bonnivochil *n* the great northern diver.

bonxie *n* the name given to the Skua gull; the common skua.

bouger, bowger *n* the puffin.

boytour *n* the bittern.

branchers *n* young crows after leaving the nest, and taking to the boughs or branches; a young bird unable to fly.

brichtie; bricht-lintie *n* the chaffinch.

bridal *n* "a craw's bridal", the designation given to a numerous flight of crows.

briskie, brisk-finch *n* the chaffinch.

brongie *n* a name given to the cormorant.

brown gled *n* the hen harrier.

buckartie-boo *v* to coo as a pigeon.

bubbly-jock *n* a turkey cock.

bulker *n* the puffin.

bull-of-the-bog *n* the bittern.

bull-fit, bullfit *n* the swift, a martin.

bull-french, bullie *n* the bullfinch.

buntlin, buntling *n* the bunting.

bur-baker *n* the water-ouzel.

burdie *n* a small bird; a young bird.

burnbecker *n* a name given to the water-ousel, and also to the water-wagtail.

burrian *n* the red-throated diver.

buter *n* the bittern.

buttermilk-gled *n* a bird of the falcon tribe.

C

cais, kais *n* jackdaws.

calaw, callaw, callow, caloo *n* the pintail duck.

capercailye, capercailzie, capercalyeane *n* the wood-grouse or mountain cock.

caper-lintie *n* the whitethroat.

cat-gull *n* the herring gull.

catyogle *n* the great horned owl.

chack, check *n* the wheatear.

chackart, chackie, chiskin, chickstane *n* the stone-chatter.

chaffie *n* the chaffinch.

charlie-mufti *n* the whitethroat.

cheepart *n* the meadow-pipit; a small person with a shrill voice.

chink *n* the reed bunting.

chirm *v* to warble.

chirme *v* used to denote the mournful sound emitted by birds, especially when collected together before a storm.

chirple *v* to twitter as a swallow.

chittle *v* to warble, to chatter, to twitter; to chirp.

chittler *n* a small bird of the titmouse species.

chucket *n* the blackbird.

chuckie *n* a hen; a chicken.

churr-muffit *n* the whitethroat.

churr-owl *n* the night-jar.

chye *n* the chaffinch.

clake, cleck, claik *n* the barnacle goose.

clatter-goose *n* the brent-goose.

clocharet *n* the stone chatter; the stonechat, *Motacilla rubicola.*

clocharch *n* the wheatear.

coal-and-candle-light *n* the long-tailed duck.

coal-hoodie *n* the black headed bunting; the reed bunting; the blackcap; the British coal titmouse.

cocks crowing *v* if cocks crow before the *Ha'-door,* it is viewed as betokening the immediate arrival of strangers.

cock-shilfa *n* the male chaffinch.

cockandie *n* the puffin.

cockrel *n* a young cock; used to denote a young male raven.

colehood *n* the black-cap.

colin-blackhead *n* the reed bunting.

colk *n* the eider duck, a sea-fowl.

coot *n* the guillemot.

corbie, corbie craw *n* the raven. "This bird, like the pyat or magpie, as well as the harmless crow, is, in the estimation of the vulgar and superstitious, a bird of evil omen".

corn-craik, -craiker *n* the land-rail, *Rallus crex*; a hand-rattle, used to frighten birds from sown seed or growing corn, denominated from its harsh sound as resembling the cry of the rail.

corn-skraugh, cornieskraugh *n* the rail, a bird.

couk *n, v* a term used to denote the sound emitted by a cuckoo.

coulter-neb *n* a sea-fowl and bird of passage; the puffin.

cowe'en, cowen-elders *n* cormorants.

craigie-heron *n* the heron.

craik *n, v* the landrail; to carry on courtship by night, under the canopy of heaven, as in "to listen to the craik in the corn".

craker, craiker *n* the rail, or corn-craik.

cran, cren *n* the crane; the heron.

crane-swallow *n* the swift.

craw *n, v* a crow; "to sit like craws in the mist", to sit in the dark.

craw-maa *n* the kittiwake.

Craw-Sunday *n* the first Sunday in March, on which crows were supposed to begin to build nests.

craw-plantin *n* a rookery.

cre-waw *n, v* a jackdaw's cry.

creepy *n* the hedge-sparrow.

crested doucker *n* the great crested grebe.

crood *v* to coo, as a pigeon; to croak, as a frog.

crooding-doo *n* a woodpigeon.

croop *v* to croak like a raven.

croupie *n* the raven, as in "ae croupie 'ill no pike out anither's een".

cucking *v* a term expressive of the sound emitted by the cuckoo.

cud-doos *n* eider ducks.

curkling *v* the sound emitted by the quail.

cushie, cushie-dow *n* the ringdove.

cuttie *n* the black guillemot.

cutty-wren *n* the wren.

cygonie *n* the stork.

D

dab *v* to peck, as birds do.

deil-tak-him *n* the yellowhammer.

deukie *n* a duckling.

deil's bird *n* the magpie.

dicky *n* the hedge-sparrow.

dike-hopper *n* the wheatear.

dilser *n* the rock or field lark. It is supposed to receive this name from its frequenting rocks on the sea-shore, and feeding on the sea-lice amongst the *dilse*, or dulce.

divie-goo *n* the black-backed gull.

diving-duck *n* the pochard, the golden-eye.

doo *n* the dove.

douker, doucker *n* a diving bird; the tufted duck; the pochard; the golden-eye; the didapper; a bather.

doukar *n* a water-fowl, also called *willie-fisher*. This seems to be the *didapper*, or *ducker*, *Colymbus auritus*.

dow *n* a dove; a pigeon.

drint *v* (used of birds) to sing, to chirp.

duck-dub, duke-dub *n* a duck-pool.

ducker *n* the cormorant.

dunter-goose *n* the eider-duck.

dykie *n* short for dyke-sparrow, a hedge-sparrow.

E

eard-titling *n* the meadow-pipit.

earl-duck *n* the red breasted merganser.

earn *n* the eagle.

earn-bleater *n* the snipe; the curlew.

ebb-sleeper *n* the dunlin.

ern *n* the eagle; the osprey.

ern-bleater *n* the snipe.

ess-cock *n* the dipper.

F

fallow-chat *n* the wheatear.

falty-flyer *n* the fieldfare.

falk *n* the razorbill.

faskidar *n* the northern gull.

faup *n* the curlew.

fearn-owl *n* the nightjar.

fedder *n* a feather.

fedderame *n* wings.

feesyhant *n* the pheasant.

feltifare *n* the redshank.

feltiflyer *n* the fieldfare.

fethir *v* to fly.

fewlume *n* the sparrow-hawk.

fiddler *n* the common sandpiper.

fire-tail, fire-tail-bob *n* the redstart.

fish-hawk, fishing-hawk *n* the osprey.

flaucht *n, v* a considerable number of birds on the wing; a spreading or a flapping of wings.

fleg *v* to fly; to flutter from place to place.

flichter *n* a great number of small objects flying in the air; the *flicht* of a winnowing-machine, as in "a flichter of birds".

flocht *n* on the wing.

flochter *v* to give free scope to joyful feelings.

flockmele *adv* in flocks.

fuffit *n* the British long-tailed titmouse.

fulmar *n* a species of petrel.

FULMAR

G

---

gae *n* the jay.

gale *n* a flock of geese.

gale *v* applied to the note of a cuckoo.

game-hawk *n* the peregrine falcon.

garb *n* a young bird; a child.

garbel *n* a young, unfledged bird.

gare, gare-fowl *n* the great auk.

garwhoungle *n* the noise of the bittern in rising from the bog.

gastrel *n* a kind of hawk; a kestrel.

gaudin *n* a semi-aquatic bird which always has its nest in the bank of a rivulet; something larger than a skylark; a bird with back and wings of a dark grey, approaching to black, the breast white, which delights to sit on large stones and islets in the middle of the water. Probably the water-crow or water-ouzel.

gawlin *n* a fowl less than a duck, regarded as a prognosticator of fair weather.

giblich *n* an unfledged crow.

gingich *n* the designation in South Uist to the person who takes the lead in climbing rocks for sea-fowl.

glaid *n* the kite.

gled, glede *n* the kite; the buzzard.

gleg-hawk *n* the sparrow-hawk.

glouk *n, v* the sound made by crows or skathies over carrion.

goarling *n* an unfledged bird, anything young.

goat-chaffer *n* the nightjar.

goit *n* a young, unfledged bird.

golden-maw *n* the glaucous gull.

golden-wren *n* the goldcrest.

goldie *n* the goldfinch; the lady-bird; a cow of a light-yellow colour; the yellow gurnard.

goldspink *n* the goldfinch.

golk *n* the cuckoo.

goo, gu' *n* a gull.

goog, gorb, gorbal, gorbel, gorblet, gordlin, goslin *n* an unfledged bird.

gor-cock *n* the redcock, or moorcock.

gorby *n* the raven.

gore-crow *n* the carrion crow.

gorglyum *n* a young bird in the nest.

gormaw, goulmaw *n* the cormorant.

gouk, gowk *n* the cuckoo.

gowdie, gowdspring *n* the goldfinch.

gowdie duck, gowndie *n* the golden-eye.

goyler *n* the arctic gull.

gray hen *n* the female of the black cock, *Tetrao tetrix*.

green lintwhite *n* the green finch.

grene-serene *n* the green finch.

ground-wren *n* the willow warbler.

guck, guik, gukkow, gowk *n* the cuckoo.

gustard *n* the great bustard.

gutter-teetan *n* the rock-pipit.

gyre falcon *n* a large hawk.

H

half-web *n* the red-necked phalarope.

half-whaup *n* the bar-tailed godwit.

harle *n* the goosander.

harley *n* the swift.

harry *v* to rob bird's nests.

havoc-burds *n* those large flocks of small birds, which fly about the field after harvest; they are of different species, though all of the linnet tribe.

hawk-studyin *v* the way hawks steadily hover over their prey before they pounce on it.

hay-bird *n* the willow warbler.

heady-craw *n* the *hoodie* crow.

heather-bleat *n* the mire snipe.

heather-cock *n* the ring ouzel.

heather-lintie *n* the linnet; the mountain linnet or twite.

heather-peep *n* a bird, said to be peculiar to the mountains of Ayrshire, which continuously emits a plaintive sound.

Heaven's hen *n* the lark.

hedder-bluter *n* the bittern.

hedge-spurgy *n* the hedge-sparrow.

hegrie *n* the heron.

hell-jay *n* the razor-bill.

hempie *n* the hedge-sparrow.

herald, herald-duck *n* the dun-diver; the diving-goose; the heron.

herd's-man *n* the common skua, thought to protect young lambs from the eagle.

herle, herral *n* the heron.

hern-bluter *n* the snipe.

herone-sew *n* properly, the place where herons build.

hill-chack *n* the ring ouzel.

hill-linty *n* the twite.

hill-plover *n* the golden plover.

hill-sparrow *n* the meadow-pipit.

hillan-piet *n* the missel-thrush.

hoarsgouk *n* the snipe; the green sandpiper.

hoddie, hoddie *n* the hooded crow; a hired mourner.

hobby *n* a kind of hawk.

Holland-duck *n* the scaup.

Holland-hawk *n* the great northern diver.

hoodit craw *n* the hooded crow; the carrion crow.

hoodock *adj* like a hoody or carrion-crow; foul and greedy.

hoody *n* the hooded crow.

hoolet *n* a young owl.

hoolie-gool-oo-oo *n, v* the cry of a owl.

horie goose *n* the brent goose.

hornie-hoolet *n* the long-eared owl.

horse-cock *n* a small kind of snipe.

horsegouk, horse-gowk *n* the green sand-piper; the snipe.

houch *n, v* the moan of the wind; to hoot as an owl.

howlet-haunted *n* frequented by owls.

huam *n* the moan of an owl in the warm days of summer.

hunting-hawk *n* the peregrine falcon.

huron *n* the heron.

hurrok *n* the brent-goose.

HARLE

I, J

jecko *n* the jackdaw.

jay-piet *n* the jay.

jay-teal *n* the common teal.

jenk-amang-the-whins *n* the linnet.

jenny-cut-throat *n* the whitethroat.

jet-tribe *n* crows.

jingle-the-key *n* the cry of the yellowhammer.

jocktie, joctibeet *n* the wheat-ear; the whin-chat; the stone-chat.

jorinker *n* a bird of the titmouse species.

K

kae-hole *n* the jackdaw's hole or nest in a tower.

katabella *n* the hen harrier.

katogle *n* the eagle-owl.

kay-wattie *n* the jackdaw.

keaw *n* the jackdaw.

keelie *n* a hawk, chiefly applied to a young one; a kestrel.

kettie-neetie *n* the dipper.

killyleepy *n* the common sand-piper.

kitt-neddy *n* the sandpiper.

kitty-wren *n* the wren.

kivan *n* a covey, such as of partridges.

knag *n* the green woodpecker.

kowshot, cushat, cushie doo *n* the ringdove.

krocket *n* the oyster-catcher.

kyob, kyobie *n* a bird's crop.

L

lady-o'-heaven's-hen *n* the wren.

lairag, lacrock, larick, lairock, laverock, lavrick *n* the lark.

lamy *n* the common guillemot.

land-tripper *n* the sandpiper.

lang-craigit heron *n* the heron.

laverock-heich *n* as high as the lark soars.

lavy *n* the foolish guillemot.

layer, lyre *n* the Manx shearwater.

lich-bird, liche-fowl *n* the nightjar.

links-goose *n* the common sheldrake.

lintie, lintie-whytie, lint-white *n* the linnet; the twite.

lipperjay *n* a jackdaw or jay.

little-doucker *n* the little grebe.

little-felty-fare *n* the redwing.

little-pickie *n* the little tern.

little-whaup *n* the whimbrel.

liverock *n* the lark.

loch-learock *n* a small grey water-bird, seen on Loch Leven; called also a *whistler*. This seems equivalent to the *lavrock*, or lark of the lake.

longie, lungie *n* the guillemot.

lorn *n* the crested cormorant.

lüin *n* the red-throated diver.

luggie, luggy *n* the horned owl.

M

maa *n* the common sea-gull.

maa-craig *n* a rock frequented by gulls.

malduck, malmock *n* the fulmar.

marleyon, marlion *n* a kind of hawk, the merlin; the sparrow-hawk; the kestrel.

marrot *n* the foolish guillemot.

martin, *n* martinis (saint) fowl; (perhaps) the ring-tail, a kind of kite.

master-pen *n* a bird's chief feather.

May bird *n* the whimbrel; a person born in May.

meg-cut-throat *n* the whitethroat.

merle *n* the blackbird.

mevies *n* the song-thrush.

meycock *n* the may-cock; the grey plover.

miller's-thumb *n* the young of the bib; the river bullhead; the goldcrest.

mire-bumper *n* the bittern.

mire-snipe *n* the snipe; an accident, misfortune, plight; a person with hard features.

mither-o'-the-mawkins *n* the little grebe; a witch; an uncanny person.

mittale, mittaine, mitten, mittan *n* a kind of hawk.

mochrum-elder, -laird *n* the cormorant.

monthly-bird *n* the fieldfare.

moon, moonie, moony *n* the goldcrest.

moor-bird *n* any bird nesting on a moor.

moor-fowl *n* red game; moor-cock.

moor-poot, moor-pout *n* the young of a moor-bird; a young grouse.

morrot *n* the guillemot; the razorbill.

mortym, morton *n* (perhaps) the common marten, martlet or house-swallow.

moss-bluter, -bummer *n* the common snipe; the bittern.

moss-cheeper *n* the marsh tit-mouse; the meadow-pipit; titlark.

moss-owl *n* the short eared owl.

moth-hawk *n* the nightjar.

mountain blackbird *n* the ring ouzel.

muffie-wren *n* the willow warbler.

muffit *n* the whitethroat.

muin *n* the goldcrest.

murre *n* the razorbill.

mussel-pecker, -picker *n* the oystercatcher.

N, O

naak *n* the great northern diver.

niddle *v* (used of birds) to bill and coo; to frisk about each other at pairing-time.

norawa'-wifie *n* the little auk.

norie *n* the puffin.

north-cock *n* the snow bunting.

northern-hareld *n* the long-tailed duck.

Norwegian teal *n* the scaup.

nun *n* the blue titmouse.

nyuckfit *n* the snipe; a name probably formed from its cry when ascending.

oat-fowl *n* the name of a small bird; the snow-bunting.

oilan-auk *n* the great northern diver.

olour *n* a herb liked by swans.

oszil *n* the ring-ousel, the merle or thrush.

oven-builder *n* the willow-warbler.

owsal, ousel *n* the blackbird.

oxe'e, ox-e'en *n* the tit-mouse, titmice.

oziger *n* the state of fowls when moulting.

P

patrick *n* the partridge.

peaseweep, peesweep *n* the lapwing.

peeack, peeak *v* to chirp.

peewit *n* the cry of the lapwing.

pee-wyt *n* the green plover or lapwing.

pegpie, peg-pie *n* the magpie.

pellile *n* the redshank.

penstraker *n* the whin-lintie, the yellowhammer.

pepe, peep *n* the chirp of a bird.

pettie *n* a sea-bird.

pew *n, v* the plaintive cry of birds; the least breath of wind or smoke; the least ripple on the sea; (applied to birds) to emit a mournful sound.

peweep, pewit *n* the lapwing.

phink *n* a species of finch.

pickmaw, pickmire *n* a bird of the gull kind; the black-headed gull.

picketernie *n* the common tern; the Arctic tern.

pickerel *n* the dunlin.

pickie-burnet *n* a young black-headed gull.

pictarnie *n* the great tern.

pictarnitie *n* the pewit or black-headed gull.

pie, piet, piot, py, pyat, pye, pyet *n* the magpie.

pirr *n* a sea-fowl with a long tail and black head, its feet not webbed; a tern's cry; a gentle breath of wind.

pitcake *n* an imitative designation for the plover.

pittil *n* some kind of fowl.

pleck-pleck *n, v* the cry of the oystercatcher.

pleengie *n* the young of the herring gull.

plevar *n* the plover.

plover's page *n* the dunlin; the jack snipe.

plumy *adj* (used of birds) feathered.

plunk *v* to emit such as a sound as the raven does.

pollie-cock *n* a turkey.

poolly-woolly *n, v* an imitative term, meant to express the cry of the curlew.

poor willie *n* the bar-tailed godwit.

potterton-hen *n* the black-headed gull.

powt *n* a pullet; young partridge.

ptarmigan *n* the white grouse.

punses, punsys *n* the three fore-toes, with the claws, of a bird of prey.

puttis *n* the young of moorfowl.

puttock *n* the buzzard.

Q

quailyie, qualyie *n* a quail.

quee-beck *n, v* the cry of a startled grouse.

queest *n* the wood pigeon.

queit, quiet *n* a species of bird.

quet *n* the guillemot.

quhaup, whaap *n* the curlew.

quhirr *n* the sound of an object moving through the air with great velocity, like a partridge or a moorfowl.

quhirr *v* to emit such a sound as that of a partridge, or moorfowl, when it takes flight.

quink *n* golden-eyed duck.

R

rade-goose *n* the barnacle goose.

raen *n* the raven.

rain-bird *n* the green woodpecker; a name given to the wood-pecker on account of the peculiar cries which they are said to emit on the approach of rain.

rain-goose *n* the red-throated diver.

rammage *n, v* the sound emitted by hawks; the warbling of birds.

rannie *n* the wren.

ratch *n* the little auk.

reest *n* a roost.

red rab *n* the robin.

ring-fowl *n* the reed bunting.

ring-necked loon *n* the great northern diver.

ring-tail *n* the hen-harrier.

rittoch *n* the greater tern.

road *v* (applied to partridges or other game) when found by the setting dogs, instead of taking wing, run along the ground before the sportsman; to follow game running in this manner.

roar *v* (used of a bird) to emit a loud cry.

rock-blackbird, -starling *n* the ring ouzel.

rock-doo *n* the wild pigeon.

rock-lintie *n* the rock-pipit.

rock-starling *n* the ring-ouzel.

rocky *n* the twite.

roist *n* a roost.

rood goose *n* the brent goose.

rook *v* to cry as a crow.

rooketty-coo *n* a pigeon's coo.

rose-lintie *n* the red-breasted linnet.

rosignell *n* the nightingale.

rotch, rotchie *n* the little auk.

rout *n* (perhaps) the brent goose.

routhurrok *n* the barnacle goose.

royston-crow *n* the hooded crow.

ruddoch, ruddock *n* the red-breast; the robin.

rye-craik *n* the land-rail.

S

sand-back *n* the sand-martin.

sand-lairag *n* the common sandpiper.

sand-lark *n* the sea-lark; the common sand-piper; the ringed plover.

sand-loo *n* the ringed plover.

sand-tripper *n* the sand-piper; the ringed-plover.

sandy laverock *n* the ringed plover.

sandy *n* the common sandpiper; the sand eel.

sandy-loo *n* the ringed plover.

sandy-swallow *n* the sand martin.

saw-bill *n* the goosander; the red breasted merganser.

scarf *n* the cormorant, also the shag.

schilderene, schidderem *n* a wild fowl.

scolder *n* the oyster-catcher.

scoot *n* the common guillemot.

scooti-allan, scouti-aulin *n* the Arctic gull.

scorey *n* the brown and white gull, when young.

scove *v* to fly equably and smoothly; (used of a bird) to poise on the wing; a hawk is said to *scove* when it flies without apparently moving its wings.

scrabe *n* the Manx shearwater.

scraber, scrabber *n* the black guillemot.

scrath *n* the cormorant.

screech-bird, -thrush *n* the fieldfare.

scuddie *n* an unfledged bird.

scurrie *n* the shag.

sea-cock *n* the puffin, the foolish guillemot.

sea-coulter *n* the puffin.

sea-crow *n* the razorbill.

sea-dovie *n* the black guillemot.

sea-goo *n* the seagull.

sea-hen *n* the common guillemot; the piper or *Trigla lyra.*

sea-lark *n* the dunlin.

sea-maw *n* the seagull.

sea-mouse, sea-peak *n* the dunlin.

sea-piet, sea-pye, sea-pyet *n* the oystercatcher.

sea-quhaup, -whaup *n* a species of gull of a dark colour.

sea-snipe *n* the dunlin.

sedge-singer *n* the sedge-warbler.

seed-bird *n* the grey wagtail; the common gull.

seed-foulie *n* the pied wagtail.

seed-lady, -lauerock, -laverock *n* the wagtail, so called from its following the plough for worms.

sereachan-aittan *n* a bird with a larger body than a large mall, of bluish colour, with a bill of carnation colour, and given to shrieking hideously; (perhaps) the name should be read *screachan-aittan*, because of its shrieking.

sewis *n* places where herons breed.

sheld-fowl *n* the common sheldrake.

shelfa, shelfy, shilfa shilfaw *n* the chaffinch.

shochad *n* the lapwing.

shore-snipe *n* the common snipe.

shore-teetan *n* the rock-pipit.

short-heeled field-lark *n* the tree-pipit.

short-heeled-lark *n* the skylark.

shoulfall *n* the chaffinch.

siller-owl *n* the barn owl.

siller-plover *n* the knot.

sinnie-fynnie *n* the black guillemot.

sirdoning *v* the singing of birds.

sirdoun *v, n* to emit a plaintive cry, as some birds do; a cry of this kind.

skaildraik, skeldrake *n* the shieldrake, or sheldrake.

skaitbird *n* the Arctic gull; Richardson's skua.

skart *n* the cormorant.

skatie-goo *n* Richardson's skua.

skeeling goose *n* the shieldrake.

skiddaw *n* the common guillemot.

skirl-crake *n* the turnstone; the sea-dotterel; the Hebridal sandpiper.

skite *n* the yellowhammer.

skittery-deacon *n* the common sandpiper.

skletaskrae *n* the dunlin.

skooi *n* a species of gull.

skout *n* the guillemot.

skrach, skrauch, skraugh, skreagh *v* (used of birds) to scream, to shriek.

skraik *v* denoting the cry of a fowl when displeased

skutock *n* the foolish guillemot.

sky-goat *n* the bittern.

sky-laverock *n* the skylark.

slee-nested *adj* (used of bird's nest) laid or hatched in a cunningly hidden nest.

sleeper *n* the dunlin.

slygoose *n* the shieldrake or shelduck.

sma'-maw *n* the common gull.

small blue-hawk *n* the merlin.

small doucker *n* the little grebe.

smeu *n* the willow warbler.

smieth *n* a bird.

smookie, smoukie *n* a bird of prey.

smooth, smeuth *n* the willow warbler.

snabbie *n* the chaffinch.

snaw-bird, -flaigh, -fleck, -flight, -fowl *n* the snow bunting.

snyth *n* the coot.

sod *n* the rock dove.

SKIRL-CRAKES

soland *n* the gannet.

spangie-hewit *n* a barbarous sport of boys to young yellowhammers.

spar-hawk *n* the sparrowhawk.

sparrow *n* the corn bunting.

sparrow-hawk *n* the merlin.

specht *n* the woodpecker.

speikintare *n* the common tern.

sperk-halk *n* the sparrow-hawk.

speug, spug, spyug *n* the house sparrow.

spink *n* the goldfinch.

spoom *v* to swoop; (used of a hawk) to dart after its prey.

spratoon *n* the red-throated diver.

sprauch *n* the sparrow.

spring *n* the music of birds.

sprog, sproug, sprug, spug, spurgie *n* the house-sparrow.

sprone *n, v* a seabird's liquid dung; (used of birds) to eject liquid dung.

sprush *v* (used of birds) to raise up the feathers.

spur-hawk *n* the sparrow-hawk.

spurgie *n* the house-sparrow; a nickname for one whose step is like the hop of a sparrow.

spurrie-how *n* the sparrow-hawk.

squatter *v* to flutter in water, as a wild duck.

stainyell *n* the wagtail.

stanchell *n* a kind of hawk; the kestrel.

stancle, steinkle *n* the wheatear; the stonechat.

stane-chack, -chacker *n* the stonechat; the whinchat; the wheatear.

stane-falcon *n* the merlin.

stane-gall, stanyel *n* the kestrel.

stane-pecker *n* the purple sandpiper; the turnstone; the stonechat.

stanel, stannel *n* the kestrel or wind-hover.

stank-hen, stankie *n* a species of water-fowl, that breeds about stanks or ponds; the moorhen.

stear *n* the starling.

steenie-pouter *n* the sandpiper.

steg *n* a gander; the male of birds such as geese and ducks.

steinkle, stinkle *n* the stonechat; the wheatear.

sterop *n* a kind of hawk.

stinkle *n* the stone-chat; the wheatear.

stobbed, stob-feathered *adj* (used of a bird) unfledged.

stock-annet *n* the common sheldrake.

stock-duck *n* the mallard; a wild duck.

stock-hawk *n* the peregrine falcon.

stock-owl *n* the eagle owl.

stock-whaup *n* the curlew.

storm-cock *n* the field-fare.

storm-finch *n* the stormy petrel.

straik *v* (used of birds) to preen feathers.

strok-annet *n* the common sheldrake.

stubble-goose *n* the graying or graylag goose.

swaagin, swagging, swaging *v* fluttering as a bird's wing.

swabie *n* the great black and white gull.

swallow *n* in Teviotdale, this harmless bird is reckoned *uncannie*, as being supposed to have a "drap o' the de'il's bluid"; in other places, it is held a lucky bird and its nest is carefully protected; and the uncanniness is attributed, for the same potent reason, to the beautiful *yorlin*.

swartback *n* the great black and white gull.

swee-swee *v* to make a chirping sound.

T

tael-duck *n* the teal.

taiste *n* the black guillemot.

tam o' cheeks, tammas, tam-mie-cheekie, tammie-noddie, tammie-norie *n* the puffin.

tammie-herl *n* the heron.

tammie-wake *n* the cock-sparrow.

tang-sparrow *n* the shore pipit.

tang-whaup *n* the whimbrel.

tanmerack *n* a bird about the size of a dove, which inhabits the tops of the highest mountains.

tappin'd, tappent *adj* tufted, crested.

taring, tarret *n* the common tern.

tarrock *n* the common tern; the Arctic tern; the kittiwake when young.

tchuchet *n* the peewit or lapwing.

teeoch *n* the lapwing.

teetick *n* the tit-lark.

teetlin *n* the meadow-pipit; the rock-pipit.

teewheep, teewhoap *n* the lapwing.

teistie, testie *n* the black guillemot.

termagant *n* the ptarmigan.

teuch, teuchit, teewhit, tewit, teuchat, tuquheit *n* the lapwing, probably meant to imitate the sound made by this bird.

teuchatie *n* a young or little lapwing.

thevis-nek *n* an imitative term formed to express the cry of a lapwing.

thirrsle, thirrsle-cock-lairig *n* the song thrush.

thistle-cock *n* the corn-bunting.

thistle-finch *n* the goldfinch.

thought-bane *n* the merrythought of a fowl.

throssil *n* the song thrush.

throstle *v* to warble.

tibbie-thiefie *n* the cry of a sandpiper.

tilliwhillie *n* the curlew.

tilling *n* the titlark.

tirma *n* the sea-pie, or oystercatcher.

tirracke, tirrik, tirrock *n* the common tern, the Arctic tern, the kittiwake when young.

titing, titling *n* the tit-lark.

titlene *n* the hedge-sparrow.

toist *n* the black guillemot.

tom-thumb *n* the willow warbler.

tommie-wake *n* the cock-sparrow.

toot, tout *v* (used of a bird) to whistle, to sing.

touchet, touchit *n* the lapwing.

treader, treeder *n* a cock; a male bird.

tree-goose *n* the barnacle-goose.

tree-speeler *n* the common creeper.

trillichan *n* the oystercatcher.

trip *n* a flock; a considerable number.

trumpie *n* the skua-gull; Richardson's skua.

tueit *n* an imitative word, expressing the short shrill cry of a small bird.

turtour *n* the turtle-dove.

tweetack *n* the rock-lark.

tyst, taiste *n* the black guillemot.

U, V, W

vran *n* the wren.

waddin o' craws *n* a large flock of crows.

wader *n* a bird, supposed to be the water-hen, or the water-rail; the heron.

waeg *n* the kittiwake.

wallachie-weit *n, v* the lapwing, from *wallach*, to wail and *weit*, a term used to denote the sound made by this bird.

wallap, wallop, wallopy-week, wallopy-weep, wallopy-weet *n* the lapwing.

waller *n* a confused crowd in a state of quick motion, as, "a waller of birds".

wallock *n* the lapwing.

waly-draigle *n* the youngest bird in a nest.

ware-cock *n* the black-cock.

water-blackbird *n* the dipper.

water-craw *n* the water-ouzel; the dipper; the coot; the great northern diver.

water-eagle *n* the osprey.

water-peggie, -pyet *n* the water-ouzel, or dipper.

water-wag, -waggie *n* the wagtail, or *Motacilla*.

watery-pleeps *n* the common sandpiper; the redshank.

weardie *n* the youngest or feeblest bird in a nest.

weerit *n* the young guillemot.

weet *n, v* the cry of a chaffinch.

weet-my-fit *n* the quail, the name seems given from its cry.

wether-bleat *n* the snipe.

whaap, whap *n* the curlew

whaup-neb, whaap-neb *n* the beak of a curlew; a periphrasis for the devil, as in "the auld whaap-neb"; *whaup-nebbit*, having a long nose like a curlew.

wheel-bird *n* the nightjar.

wheeple *v* to whistle like a whaup; to whistle a shrill melancholy note, as plovers.

wheet-ah *n* the cry of the tern.

wheetie-wheet *n* a very young bird.

wheetie, wheetie-whitebeard *n* the whitethroat.

wheetle-wheetle *n* the sharp

peeping sound made by young birds.

wheetle *n* a duckling.

whew, whe-ew *v* to whistle shrilly as plovers do.

whey-beard *n* the whitethroat.

whey-bird *n* the wood-lark.

whiddle *v* to proceed with light, rapid, motion; to flutter as birds at pairing-time.

whin-chaker *n* the whin-chat.

whin-lintie *n* the linnet.

whin-sparrow *n* the field or mountain sparrow, probably denominated from its being often found among the whins or furze.

whinny *v* to cry as a snipe or a lapwing.

whipple *v* to utter short, sharp cries, as a plover or curlew.

whir, whirry away *v* to fly off with such noise as a partridge or moorcock makes when it springs from the ground.

whirky *v* to fly with a whizzing sound, like a startled partridge.

whishie *n* the whitethroat.

whistling-duck *n* the coot.

whistling-plover *n* the golden plover.

white aboon-glade *n* the hen harrier.

white-horned owl *n* the long-eared owl.

white-lintie *n* the whitethroat.

white-maw *n* the herring gull.

white-wren *n* the willow warbler.

whitterick *n* the curlew.

whunlintie *n* this is said to be the red linnet, and to be thus denominated from often building its nest among whins.

whur-cocks *n* a call given when game birds rise.

wicker *v* to whiz through the air; to flutter as a bird.

willick *n* the common guillemot; the puffin; the razor-bill; a young heron.

willie fisher *n* the sea-swallow, *Sterna hirundo*; this name is given to a waterfowl, also called a *doukar.*

willie-gow *n* the herring gull.

willie-muflie *n* the willow warbler.

willie-wagtail *n* the water wagtail.

willie-whae *v* to make the cry of the curlew.

willie-whaup *n* the curlew.

willie-whip-the-wind *n* the kestrel.

windcuffer *n* the name given to the kestrel.

wirr *v* to fly like a startled partridge.

witch-hag *n* the swallow.

witchuck *n* the sandmartin.

witherty-weep *n* the plover.

wood-thrush *n* the mistle thrush.

wran, wrannie, wrannock *n* the wren.

wrig *n* the young or feeblest bird in the nest.

wullie-wagtail *n* the water-wagtail; the pied wagtail.

X,Y,Z

yaldran, yaldrin, yallieckie *n* the yellowhammer.

yaupit *n* the blue titmouse.

yawp *n* the cry of a sickly bird, or of one in distress.

yeld kittiwake *n* a species of kittiwake so called from its neither breeding nor frequenting the breeding-places.

yeldrick, yeldring, yeldrin, yellow-yeldrick, yellow-yorlin *n* the yellowhammer.

yellow plover *n* the golden plover.

the long-necked yerl *n* the red-breasted merganser.

yerlin, yirlin *n* the yellowhammer.

yirn *n* the eagle.

yite *n* the yellow bunting; the yellowhammer.

yoldrin, yollin, yorlin, youl-ring *n* the yellowhammer.

yolpin *n* an unfledged bird.

youkfit, yuckfit, youkfit *n* the snipe.

Part five

Water

A

abone broe, aboon-bree *phr* above water; a person in difficulty, or one who is on a small income, it is commonly said, "he can hardly keep his head abone-broe".

achen, aiken *n* a small bivalve found in sandy bays.

aer, aar, air *n* a stony pebbly beach; also a smooth beach; the sea shore.

affrug o' the sea *n* a spent wave receding from the shore.

aiker *v* the motion, break, or movement made in the water by a fish when swimming away rapidly.

aikie-guineas *n* a name given by children to small flat shells, bleached by the sea.

ana, anay *n* a river-island; a holm.

andoo *v* to keep a boat in position by rowing gently against the wind.

arby *n* the sea-gilliflower, or sea-pink.

aspait *adv* in flood.

aswim *adj, adv* afloat; covered in water.

auld gibbie *n* the common cod.

awaydrawing *v* (applied to a stream of water) the act of drawing off, or turning aside.

awmucks *n* a kind of fish that have the power of inflating their bodies, there are *ling-awmucks*, *skate-awmucks* etc.

B

badderlocks, batherlocks *n* an edible seaweed resembling the hart's-tongue fern.

baggie, baggie-mennon, bag-mennon, bagrel *n* a large minnow.

bairdie *n* the loach; the three-spined stickleback.

baivee *n* a kind of whiting.

ballingar *n* a type of ship.

bane-prickle *n* the stickleback.

bang *v* to push off with a boat, in salmon fishing, without having seen any fish in the channel.

bannag *n* a white-trout; a sea-trout.

bannet-fluke *n* the turbot, so called for resembling a bonnet.

bannock-fluke *n* the name given to the genuine turbot, from its flat form as resembling a cake.

banstickle, banty *n* the three-spined stickleback or minnow.

batward *n* a boatman; literally a boatkeeper.

beardie-lotch, beardie-lowrie, beardoc *n* the loach.

bebbing-full *adj* (used of the tide) high, full.

beck *n* (perhaps) a brook or rivulet.

being, bing *n* the beach of the sea-shore.

belks *n* the stems of seaweed, formerly used to make kelp.

bellware *n* seaweed, of which kelp was made.

belth *n* (perhaps) a whirlpool or rushing of waters.

ben *n* a kind of small salmon, generally from seven to ten pounds in weight.

bergle, bergel *n* the wrasse.

bessy-lorch *n* the fish called a loach.

bing *n* the sea-beach.

birlin *n* a long-oared boat of the largest size, often with six, sometimes with eight oars, generally used by the chieftains in the Western Isles.

birth *n* a current in the sea, caused by a furious tide but taking a different course from it.

black-fish *n* newly-spawned fish; a salmon after spawning.

black-tang *n* the ore-weed; seaweed.

bland-hoe, blind-hoe *n* the rabbit fish.

bleis *n* the name given to a river fish.

bleuchan *n* a small, salt-water fish of some kind.

blibbans *n* strips of soft, slimy matter, seaweed on rocks at ebb-tides; large shreds of greens or cabbages put into broth.

blind-fish *n* the lesser-spotted dogfish.

bluchans *n* name given to those small fish which children catch in rock pools.

boatie *n* a yawl, or small boat.

bobbins *n* the water-lily.

bod *adj* the fretting of the sea on the shore.

bodach *n* the small-ringed seal; a spectre; a hobgoblin; an old man; a name for the devil.

boddum-lyer *n* a large trout that keeps to a bottom of a pool.

bog-war *n* tangles and other seaweeds with balls or bladders on the fronds.

bonnet-fleuk *n* the pearl, a fish.

bosum *n* inlet loch: applied to the sea-lochs on the West of Scotland.

bourbee *n* the spotted whistle-fish.

boxie-vrack *n* the seaweed *Fucus pixidatus.*

brack *n* a flood, when the ice breaks in consequence of a thaw; a sudden and heavy fall of rain.

braggir *n* a coarse seaweed; the broad leaves of marine algae.

braise *n* the roach, a fish of the genus *Pagrus vulgaris.*

brandstickle *n* the stickleback.

brannock *n* a young salmon.

branstickle *n* the three-spined stickleback.

brassy, bressie *n* the fish wrasse or "old wife".

brim, brym *adj* (applied to the sea) raging, swelling; border, or margin of a river, lake or sea.

brus *v* to foam or roar like the sea.

buckie *n* the sea-snail, or its shell; any spiral shell; a periwinkle; a trifle of no regard.

buckie-ingram *n* the crab.

buckie-prin *n* a periwinkle.

bukat *n* a male salmon.

buller *v* to emit such a sound as water does, when rushing violently into any cavity, or forced back again.

burn *n* water, particularly that which runs from a fountain or a well; a rivulet, a brook.

burn the water *phr* a phrase used to denote the act of killing salmon with a *lister* by torch-light.

burn-brae *n* the acclivity at the bottom of which a rivulet runs.

burn-grain *n* a small rill running into a larger stream.

burnmen *n* water-carriers; also called *burn-leaders*: men who carried water from burns and wells to supply the brewers, dyers, skinners etc. in a manufacturing town.

burnside *n* the ground situated on the side of a rivulet.

buss *n* a sunken rock on which at very low tides seaweed is visible, like a bush; a small ledge of rocks projecting into the sea, covered with seaweed.

bykat *n* a male salmon.

C

ca' o' the water *phr* the motion of the waves as driven by the wind; the waves drive towards the west, as in "the ca' of the water is west".

caain *v, n* the driving of whales into shallow water; a drove of whales.

caaing-whale *n* the *Delphinus deductor.*

cairbran *n* the basking shark.

caithie *n* a large-headed fish.

caizie *n* a fishing boat.

calf-skins *n* the sea ruffled by the wind in occasional spots.

calm *adj* (used of ice) smooth, even.

camdui *n* a species of trout.

canare *n* a water-bailiff.

candavaig *n* a foul salmon that has lain in fresh water till summer, without going to the sea; a peculiar species of salmon.

canniburr, canniber *n* the sea-urchin.

cap *v* to direct one's course at sea.

carbin, cairban, carfin *n* the basking shark.

cardui *n* a species of trout in Loch Leven, probably the char. It is round-shouldered, the most beautiful in colour of all the trout species in our waters. Without scales, dark olive on the back, the

CAIZIE

sides spotted, the belly a livid red, and the underfins of a beautiful crimson edged with a snow white. It is a rare fish.

carfin *n* the basking shark.

carling *n* the name of a fish, the pogge.

cat-strand *n* a very small stream.

caver *n* a gentle breeze moving the water slightly.

chaffer *n* the round-lipped whale.

claddach, cleddach *n* a shingly beach.

clidyoch, clydyoch *n* the gravel bed of a river.

clubbock *n* the spotted blenny, a fish.

clunkertonie *n* a jellyfish, *medusa*.

co *n* a rock cave, with a narrow entrance, on the sea shore.

coble *n* a short, flat-bottomed boat, used in salmon-fishings and in ferries; a pond for cattle etc. to drink at.

cog *n* a yawl or cockboat.

colemie *n* the coalfish.

cominie *n* a young coal-fish.

coudle *v* to float; as a feather

alternately rising and sinking with the waves.

cove *n* a cave; a sea-cave; also applied to a narrow inlet or recess on a steep rocky coast.

cowan *n* a fishing boat.

craig-flook *n* the rock flounder.

crap o' the water *n* the first water taken from a well after midnight of December 31st, supposed to bring luck for the new year.

craw-pockies *n* the eggs of sharks, skates and dog-fish.

crowner *n* the name of a fish.

cruve, cruive *n* a box resembling a hen-crib placed in a dam or dike that runs-across a river, for confining the fish that enter into it.

cuddie *n* a ditch or cutting to lead the drainage of a district to a river; also, an overflow connection between a canal and a river.

cungles *n* course gravel; roundish water-worn stones.

curglaff *n* the shock felt in bathing, when one first plunges into cold water.

currach, currok *n* a skiff or small boat.

cuth *n* a coal-fish, not fully grown.

D

daberlack *n* a kind of long seaweed.

deadman's-paps *n* the star-fish.

deep *n* the deepest part of the river.

deil's pots and pans *n* holes in the bed of a stream, caused by stones carried down and boiling in flood-time.

dew *adj* moist.

dib, dub *n* a small pool of rainwater.

doach, doagh *n* a salmon-weir or cruive.

doksilver *n* dock-dues, harbour-dues.

doister *n* a storm from the sea.

donal'-blue *n* the jelly-fish.

drizzle *n* a little water in a rivulet scarce appearing to run.

drow *n, v* a melancholy sound, like that of the dashing waves heard at a distance.

dubby *adj* abounding with small pools, puddles; wet, rainy.

duck-dub, duke-dub *n* a duck-pool.

dulse *n* a common species of edible seaweed.

dunter *n* the porpoise.

E

ebb *adj* shallow, not deep.

ebbness *n* shallowness.

ebb-mother *n* the last of the ebb tide.

ebb-stone *n* a rock exposed at ebb-tide.

eela *n* a fishing place, or ground for fishing, near the shore.

eel-beds *n* the water crowfoot.

eeram *n* a boat-song; a rowing song.

eve-eel, evil-eel *n* the conger eel.

F

fall *v* to sink; to subside.

fa'in *v* "the water's sair fa'in in", the river has subsided much.

feyadin *n* the whale.

fierd *n* a ford.

fiery-flaw *n* the sting-ray.

fiery-tangs *n* the crab.

fiery-water *n* marine phosphorescence.

fleet-water *n* water which overflows ground.

fleit *n, v* overflowing of water.

flese-wilk *n* the striated whelk.

finner *n* a species of whale.

finnie *n* a salmon not a year old.

finnack, finnock *n* a white trout, in colour and shape like a salmon.

fish-carle *n* a fisherman.

fish-currie *n* any deep hole or secret recess, in a river, in which the fishes hide themselves.

fire-bit, fire-burn *n* marine phosphorescence.

flews *n* a sluice for turning water off an irrigated meadow.

flodden *v* flooded.

flosh *n* a swamp; a body of standing water.

floshin, floshan *n* a puddle of water, larger than a *dub*, but shallow.

flothis *n* a flood.

flouss *n* a flood.

flow *n* a watery moss; a low-lying piece of rough, watery land, not broken up.

fluff *n* a sea anemone.

fluke *n* a flounder.

flusch *n* a run of water; snow in a state of dissolution: this in Scotland is commonly named *slush*.

flushy *adj* (used of ice on the surface of a lake) thawing.

fluther *n* rise in a river, so as to discolour the water, though not so great as a speat.

flyam *n* a large seaweed tangle, growing round the shore.

fogrie *n* the mackerel.

follieshat *n* the jelly-fish.

forking *n* the division of a river into one or more streams; a branch of a river at its parting from the main body.

fors *n* a cascade, a waterfall.

forth *n* an inlet of the sea.

fyke *n* the fish, Medusa's head.

G

gairfish *n* the porpoise.

gallytrough *n* the chard.

gakie *n* *Venus mercenaria*, a shell.

gaar, garr *n* vegetable substance in the bed of a river.

gawkie *n* the horse-cockle shell, *Venus islandica*.

ged *n* the pike.

gerrack *n* a coal-fish of the first season.

gerron *n* a sea-trout.

ginnel *n* a runlet or narrow channel for water; a street gutter, as in "bairns like to plouter in the ginnels".

gilse *n* a young salmon.

ginnelin, ginnle *v* to fish with the hands by groping under banks and stones.

gio *n* a deep ravine which admits the sea.

gipsy herring *n* the pilchard.

glassock *n* the coal-fish.

gleshan *n* the coal-fish.

glog-rinnin *adj* (used of a river) running slowly, dark and deep.

glotten *n, v* a partial thaw, in consequence of which the water begins to appear in the ice; a river is said to have got a *glottenin* when a little swelled as above described.

goat, got, gote *n* a narrow cavern or inlet, into which the sea enters; a small trench; a slough etc.

goe *n* a creek.

goor *v* (used of streams) to become choked with masses of ice and snow in a thaw.

gray fish *n* the coal fish.

graylord *n* the coal fish full grown.

graulse, grawl *n* a young salmon.

great *adj* (applied to a body of running water) swelled with rain.

grilse *n* a salmon not fully grown.

ground ebb *n* extreme low water; the lower part of the foreshore.

groo, gree, gruse *n* the

designation given to water, when passing from the liquid state to that of ice; water only part congealed.

groo up *v, adj* water is said to be *groo'd up* when it is chocked up by ice in a half-congealed state.

grudge *v, adj* applied to water interrupted in its course, then said to be *grudg'd up.*

grund-grue *n* water beginning to congeal, at the lower part of a stream.

gruse *n* half-frozen water.

guard-fish *n* the sea pike.

guddle, gudge *v* to catch fish with the hands, by groping under the stones or banks of a stream.

gunner flook *n* the turbot.

gun-plucker *n* a kind of fish with a wide mouth.

gurd *v* (applied to running water when stopped in its course by earth, ice etc) to stop.

gurl *n* a place where the stream, being confined by rocks, issues with rapidity, making a gurgling noise.

gushel *n* the name given to that small dam which is made in a gutter or streamlet in order to intercept the water. It is applied both to the dams made by children for amusement and to those made by masons, plasterers etc. for preparing their lime or mortar.

H

haaf *n* the sea, as distinguished from inlets, or fishing-ground on the coast: the term is equivalent to *the deep sea.*

haaf-eel *n* conger eel.

haaf-fish *n* the great seal.

haaf-seat *n* a deep sea fishing ground.

haaf fishing, haafing *v* deep sea fishing.

haddag, haddie *n* a haddock.

haddock-sand *n* sea-ground frequented by haddocks.

haf, haff *n* the deep sea.

hairy-hutcheon *n* the sea-urchin.

hank *n* the lee side of a boat.

hard-head *n* the grey gurnard; the father-lasher; a kind of sea-scorpion.

harley *n* a harbour.

heavinning place *n* a harbour.

herbery, herbry, harbory *n* a haven or harbour.

herring drewe *n* a school of herring.

hewin *n* a haven or harbour.

hill-burn *n* a mountain stream.

hilly *adj* (used of the sea) rough, heaving, having huge waves.

hope *n* a small bay.

hose-fish *n* the cuttle-fish.

huddum *n* a kind of whale.

hurlygush *n* the bursting out of water, as in "what an awfu' hurly-gush the pond made".

hush *v* a swell or rolling motion of the sea.

I

ile *n* the fishing ground inside the main tidal current, in the space between two points where there is a counter-current.

inscales *n* the racks at a lower end of a *cruive* in a river.

insh *n* low-lying land near a river.

inundit, inundate *adj* inundated, flooded.

inver *n* the mouth of a stream or a river; the confluence of a river.

jabble *v, n* a slight motion of water; a slight agitation of the waters of the sea with the wind; small irregular waves, and running in all directions.

jagger-steamer *n* a steamer for the transportation of herrings.

jap *v* (used of water) to dash waves; to splash.

japper *n* a hollow, broken wave.

jawp *v* (used of water) to dash and rebound; to play fast and loose, as in "to jawp waters"; "I'll no' jawp waters wi' you", said to a person who has made a bargain with another, and wishes to cast it.

jevel *n* the dashing of water.

jingle *n* the smooth water at the back of a stone in the river.

jaw-hole *n* a place into which dirty water etc. is thrown.

jow *v* (used of a river) to roll forcibly in flood; the dashing of a wave on the shore.

jumm *n, v* that deep hollow sound which comes from the rocks on the sea-shore, during a storm, when the ocean is highly agitated; caused partly by the waves, and partly by the hurling pebbles, striking the rocks.

jurr *n, v* the noise of a small waterfall descending among stones and gravel.

jurram *n* a slow and melancholy boat song.

K

kaner, kainer *n* overseer; bailiff; water-bailiff.

kair *n* a mire; a puddle.

keechan *n* a small rivulet.

keeling, keling, keiling, killing, killin *n* cod of a large size.

keething-sight *n* the view of the motion of a salmon, by marks in the water.

kelpie *n* the spirit of the waters, who, as is vulgarly believed, gives previous intimation of the destruction of those who perish within his jurisdiction, by preternatural lights and noises, and even assists in drowning them.

kettach *n* the fishing-frog or sea devil.

kiltie *n* a spawned salmon.

klack *n* fishing ground near the shore, as opposed to *haff*.

krang *n* the body of a whale divested of blubber.

L

laager *n* the halibut.

labb *n, v* the sound of lapping waves.

lade, laid *n* the watercourse leading to a mill.

laik *n* (perhaps) a shallow part of the sea, where the tides are irregular.

lammas-stream *n* a strong and high spring-tide in August.

lamp o' the water *n* phosphorescence on the sea.

lamper eel *n* the lamprey.

lane *n* a brook, of which the motion is so slow as to be scarcely perceptible.

lang sang *n, v* a noise made by the waves on the bar of a harbour.

lapster *n* a lobster.

lavellan *n* a kind of weasel; a mythical creature living in lakes, etc. and squirting poison to a great distance.

lax *n* a salmon.

le, lee *n* the water of the sea in motion.

lempit *n* a limpet.

lempit-ebb *n* the shore between high and low tide, where limpets are gathered.

leth *n* a channel, or small run of water.

lin *v* to hollow out of the ground by force of water.

lingy *adj* applied to the greasy surface that settles on stagnant water.

linn *n* the precipice over which water falls; the cascade of water; the pool at the base of the fall.

lipper *n* a slight swell or ruffle on the surface of the sea; a ripple; a wavelet; to rise and fall gently on the waves.

lipperis *n* the tops of broken waves.

lobster-toad *n* the deep-sea crab, the *Cancer araneus*.

laugh *n* a loch.

loch-head *n* the head of a loch.

loch-liver *n* a jelly-fish.

loch-lubbertie *n* sea-fallen stars.

lochan *n* a small loch.

loddan, lodden *n* a small pool.

loop *n* the winding of a river, lake or glen; the channel of a stream left dry by the water changing its course.

loup, loupe *n* a small cataract, which fishes attempt to leap over; a place where a river becomes so contracted that a person may leap over it.

louper-dog *n* the porpoise.

lucky's-lines *n* a plant growing in deep water near the shore.

lucky-words *n* words which Shetland fishermen only use during deep-sea fishing.

luf and lie *v* a sea term, to hug the wind closely.

M, N, O

mallachie *adj* of a milk and water colour.

mallow *n* the sea-wrack.

malm *v* to soften and swell by means of water; to steep; to become mellow.

maze of herring, mese of herring *n* five hundred herrings.

menoun *n* a minnow.

mere *n* the sea; an arm of the sea; a small pool caused by the moisture of the soil, often one that is dried up by the heat.

mereswine *n* a dolphin.

mermaid's glove *n* the sponge.

minn *n* a straight between two islands with a strong current.

moder-dy, -sook *n* a current setting in towards the land.

mountain-spate *n* a mountain-torrent

neapit *adj* (used of tides) low.

needlach *n* a small, young eel.

nicker *n* a water-sprite.

nine-eyed-eel *n* the less lamprey.

nissac *n* a porpoise.

nixie *n* a water-nymph.

noust *n* a landing place for a boat, especially where the entrance is rocky; a sort of ditch in the shore, into which a boat is drawn for being moored.

numb *adj* of a boat, slow in sailing, almost motionless.

o'erswak *n, v* the rush or noise of a wave breaking on the beach.

o'er-loup, overloup *n* the stream-tide at the change of the moon.

outrook, outrug *n* the backward wash of a wave after breaking.

outshot *n* ebb-tide.

oyse *n* an inlet of the sea.

MERESWINE

P

paddle *n* the lump-fish.

paddock-rude *n* the spawn of frogs.

pallach *n* a porpoise.

pallawa *n* a species of sea-crab.

partan *n* common sea crab.

pasper, paspie *n* samphire.

pearl shell *n* the pearl mussel.

peat-bree, -brew, -broo *n* peaty water.

peeriweerie, peerie-weerie *n* a slow-running stream.

pellack, pellock *n* a porpoise.

pew *n, v* the plaintive cry of birds;

the least breath of wind or smoke; the least ripple on the sea.

peyailack *n* the membranous covering of the roe of a fish, the entire roe.

phinoc *n* a species of grey trout.

piew *n* a very faint breath of wind or ripple on water.

pile *n* the motion of the water made by a fish when it rises to the surface.

pinking *v* a word expressive of the sound of a drop of water falling in a cave.

pintill-fish *n* the pipe-fish, or the launce.

pirl *v* to be gently rippled, as the surface of water by a light wind.

plash *v* to make a noise by dashing water; applied to anything which, from being thoroughly drenched, emits the noise occasioned by the agitation of water.

plash-fluke *n* the fish called plaice.

plum, plumb *n, v* a deep pool in a river or stream; the designation might arise from the practice of measuring a deep body of water with a *plumb*-line; the noise a stone makes when plunged into a deep pool.

plype *v* to paddle or dabble in water; to fall into water.

pod *n* (perhaps) a toad.

poddock *n* a frog.

podle *n* a tadpole.

podlie *n* the fry of the coal-fish; the green-backed pollack; the true pollack.

pollachie *n* the crab-fish.

pooty *n* a small cod.

pou, pow *n* a pool; a slow-moving rivulet in flat lands; a watery or marshy place; a small creek, affording a landing base for boats; the wharf itself.

pouk *n* a little pit or hole containing water or mire.

powart *n* a seal.

preeve *v* to stop at any place at sea, in order to make trial for fish.

pricker *n* the basking shark.

prickly-tang *n* the *Fucus serratus*.

puddock *n* a frog.

puddock-pony *n* a tadpole.

pue *n* a faint breath of wind or ripple on water.

pulloch *n* a young crab.

punger *n* a species of crab.

purle *n* a pearl.

quhite fisch *n* the name given to haddocks, ling etc.

R

race *n* a current; a course at sea; freight of water from a well.

rack *n* a very shallow ford, of considerable breadth.

raise-net *n* a net that falls and rises with the tide.

rak, rawk *n* the greenish scum on stagnant water.

raiss *n* a strong current in the sea.

rampar eel *n* a lamprey.

range *v* to agitate water by plunging, for the purpose of driving fish from their holds.

randon *v* to flow swiftly in a straight line.

rannok flook *n* a species of flounder.

rattar ebb *n* a stream ebb, as shewing the *red ware*.

raun, rawn *n* the roe or spawn of a fish; a female fish, as a salmon or herring.

raun-fleuk, rawn-fleuk *n* the turbot.

rauner *n* the female salmon which has the roe.

ravel-lock *n* a kind of river-lock.

reaming-calm *n* a calm with the sea smooth as cream.

reb *n* a large tract of fishing ground.

red *n* the spawning ground; (used of fish) in the spawning state.

red-belly *n* the char.

red-ware *n* sea girdles.

red-ware cod *n* cod of a red colour.

red-ware fishick *n* the whistle-fish.

rede fische *n* salmon in the state of spawning.

redware *n* sea-girdles, seaweeds growing in shallow waters.

ree *n* an enclosure from a river or the sea, open towards the water, to receive small vessels; a harbour.

reeds *n* a method of catching the young coal-fish with a hand-line from a boat anchored near the shore.

reegh, reigh *n* a harbour.

reid fische *n* fish in a spawning state.

reyd *n* a road for ships.

rice the water *v* to throw plants or branches of trees into a river, for frightening the salmon, before using the lister; the effect is that they become stupid and lie motionless.

ride *n* the current or swell of the sea.

rill *n* a small stream.

rim *n* a rocky bottom in the sea.

rin *n* a run; a waterfall, also a stream, as in "a rin of water"; a ford, where the water is shallow, and ripples as it flows.

rink *n* the course of a river.

rinlet *n* a small stream.

rive *n* shallows.

roaring-buckie *n* a kind of seashell, the common whelk, *Buccinum undatum.*

rockman *n* a cragsman who catches sea-fowl.

rodden-fleuk *n* the turbot.

rodding-time *n* spawning-time.

rone *n* a run or sheet of ice.

roun *n* roe of fish.

roust, roost, rost *n* a strong tide or current.

routing-well *n* a well that makes a rumbling sound, predicting a storm.

rowan *n* a turbot.

ruiff *n* running water; streams.

ruthaig *n* a large, edible crab.

S

sab *n* the noise of the sea.

saedick *n* a place frequented by fish.

saelkie *n* a seal; a sea-calf; a big stout person.

saed, saet, said, saithe *n* a full-grown coal-fish.

saftie *n* a shore-crab that has cast its shell.

sail-fish *n* the basking shark.

sally, saully *n, v* a continuous rising and falling; a sail in a small boat over rough water; the swinging or bounding motion of a ship at sea.

salt se, sea *n* the sea.

san', sand *n* a sandy-bottomed fishing ground.

sand-eel *n* the sand-lance.

sand-fleuk *n* the smear-dab.

sand-louper, -lowper *n* sand-hopper; a small species of crab.

sandy-giddack *n* the launce.

sannal *n* the sand eel.

saut-bree *n* salt water.

saut-water *n* the sea, the sea-side.

saylch *n* a seal; a sea-calf.

saxear *n* a six-oared boat.

sca'd-man's-head *n* the sea-urchin's shell.

scantack *n* a fishing-line fixed on the bank of a stream for night-fishing.

scap *n* a bed of mussels.

scaud-man's-head *n* sea-urchin.

scaup *n* a bed or stratum of shell-fish, as in "an oyster scaup".

scriddan *n* a mountain torrent.

scringing *v* fishing at night with small nets and no torches.

scummer *n* the boy who in a herring boat catches the fish that drop from the net when being hauled; the poke-net on the end of a pole by which he catches the falling fish.

scur *n* a small fresh-water fish.

scuttal *n* a pool of filthy water; a *jaw-hole*.

sea fallen stars, sea lungs *n* an animal thrown on the sea shore in summer and autumn; *Medusa aequorea*, or sea-nettle.

sea-breach *n* a breaker.

sea-bree *n* the waves of the sea.

sea-broken *adj* shipwrecked.

sea-candle *n* the phosphorescence of the sea.

sea-cat *n* the wolf-fish.

sea-daisy *n* the thrift.

sea-edge *n* the margin of the sea.

sea-fike *n* the name given to a marine plant, which, when rubbed on the skin, causes itchiness.

sea-fire, -light *n* the phosphorescence of the sea.

sea-growth *n* the names given, by fishermen to various species of *sertulariae, flustrae* etc. which are attached to small stones, shells etc.

sea-haar *n* a sea-fog.

sea-hack *n* a temporary thaw occasioned by the salt vapour during the rising tide.

sea-light *n* the phosphorence of the sea.

sea-maiden *n* a mermaid.

sea-meath, -meeth *n* a landmark to those out at sea.

sea-pellock *n* the porpoise.

sea-pheasant *n* the turbot.

sea-poacher *n* the armed bull-head; the pogge, a fish.

sea-spire *n* sea-spray.

sea-swine *n* the wrasse.

sea-trowe *n* a marine goblin.

sea-waur *n* algae thrown up by the sea, used as manure.

sea-worm *n* a crab.

sealch, sealgh *n* a seal; a sea-calf.

sealch's-bubble *n* a jelly-fish.

seath *n* the coal fish.

seep-sabbin' *v* the sound of dripping, trickling water, or of a brook.

seip *v, n* to ooze; to leak; to soak through; a leakage; a puddle; a state of wetness; a small spring or stream of water.

seipin *adj* very wet; dripping.

selcht *n* a seal.

sellag *n* the fry of the coal-fish.

sellock *n* a fish.

seth, sey *n* the coal-fish.

Setterdayis slop *n* a gap ordained to be left in the cruives for catching salmon, in fresh waters, from Saturday after the time of Vespers, till Monday after sunrise.

shall *n* a shell.

shall *v* to speak or 'leister' salmon in shallow water.

shank *v* (used of a stream) to join another.

shaul, shawl *adj* shallow; as in the proverb "shawl water maks mickle din".

shedder-salmon *n* a female salmon just after spawning.

shelf *n* a rock or reef under water.

shelky *n* a seal; a sea-calf.

shelly-coat *n* a spirit, supposed to reside in the waters.

shoggle *n* a large piece of ice floating down a river after the ice is broken up.

Shony *n* the name formerly given to a marine deity worshipped in the Western Isles.

shoremil *n* the margin of the sea.

shot *n* the spot where fishermen are wont to let out their nets; the sweep of a net; the draught of fishes made by a net.

showd *n, v* (applied sometimes to the motion of a ship tossed by the waves) a rocking motion.

shud, shude *n* a large body of ice; broken pieces of ice, especially in a floating state, as in "shudes of ice".

shull *n* a shoal.

shullie *n* a small shoal.

sight *n* a station whence fishers observe the motion of salmon in the river.

sight *v* to spy fish in the water from

the banks, in order to direct the casting of the net.

sike *n* a small rill; a marshy bottom or hollow with one or more small streams.

sile *n* the young of herring.

sillar sawnies *n* periwinkles, common shells on shores.

sillik, sillak, sellok *n* the fry of the coal-fish.

sipe, seip *n* a slight spring of water; the moisture which comes from any wet substance.

skaab *n* the bottom of the sea.

skaffe *n* a small boat.

skail *n, v* the noise of waves breaking on the shore.

skail-water *n* the superfluous water that is let off by a sluice before it reaches the mill.

skares *n* rocks in the sea.

skate-rings *n* jelly-fish.

skeetack, skeetick, skeetie *n* the cuttle-fish.

skelly *n* the chub.

skelly-coat *n* a water-sprite.

skiuldr *n* the jelly-fish, *Medusa.*

skleff *adj* shallow.

skoodra *n* the ling.

skool *n* a shoal of fish.

skoorie *n* coal-fish fully grown.

skorit *n* (applied to a ship) wreck.

skule, skull *n* a great collection of individuals, such as fishes.

skulp *n* the sea-jelly.

skurr *n* a small spot of fishing ground.

skyr *n* a rock in the sea.

slake, slaik, sleegh, sloke *n* the oozy vegetable substance in the bed of rivers.

slawk *n* a slimy plant, which grows in burns and springs.

sleech *n* silt; sea-wrack; the oozy vegetable substance found in riverbeds; foreshores on which silt is deposited by the tide.

sletch *n* slime, particularly that in the beds of rivers, or on the sea-shore.

slieve-fish *n* the cuttle-fish.

slike *n* river bed ooze.

sloum *n* the green scum that gathers on stagnant pools.

smelt *n* a smooth spot on the sea.

smolt, smelt, smelte, smout *n* the fry of salmon.

sniggle *v* to poach fish by snaring them in a mean way.

snuain *n* a seaweed.

sockin of the tide *n* the last of the tide, either of the ebb or flood.

solefleuk *n* the sole.

soom *v* to swim, to float; to cause to float.

sough o' the sea *n* "the sound of the sea, as the sea begins to speak before the sky. As the sea doth thus growl, farewell to fair weather for a while."

soume *v* to swim.

spait *n* a flooding; a sudden rush of water.

spait-ridden *adj* carried along by a flood.

spathie *n* the spotted river-trout.

spire *n* the spray of the sea.

spirling *n* a small burn trout.

splash fluke *n* the plaice, a flat fish.

spout *n* the razor fish.

spout-whale *n* a name given to the porpoise.

squash *v* to splash; to dash water; to fall heavily into water.

squatter *v* to flutter in water, as a wild duck.

squaw-hole *n* a broad, shallow, muddy pond.

squeem *n* the motion of a fish as observed by its motion in the water.

squeesh *n, v* the sound of water suddenly poured out.

staners *n* the small stones and gravel on the margin of a river or lake; those within the channel of the river, which are occasionally dry.

stang *n* the shorter pipe-fish.

stank *n* a pool or pond; the ditch of a fortified town.

stank-lochen *n* a stagnant lake.

stanked *adj* surrounded by a ditch.

stanners *n* the gravelly shores of a river.

stanner-steps, step-stanes *n* stepping-stones laced across the bed of a stream.

steethe-stone *n* the first of the stones set down as an anchor to deep-sea fishing lines.

stein-biter *n* a lump-fish.

stell *n* a deep pool in a river, where nets for catching salmon are placed.

stem *n* the name given in Caithness to a sort of enclosure made with stones on the side of a river, into which salmon are driven.

stenloch *n* an overgrown seath or coal-fish.

sting *v* (applied to a boat) to push it forward, or across a river, by means of a pole.

stoer-mackrel *n* the tunny fish.

stone-fish *n* the spotted blenny.

storm water *n* surface water.

stour *n* a gush of water; the spray driven, in consequence of the agitation of water.

strand, stran' *n* a stream; a rivulet; a gutter; a channel or drain for water.

strath *n* a valley of considerable extent, through which a river runs; a country confined by hills on two sides of a river.

strick *n* "strick o' the watter", the most rapid part of any stream.

strict *adj* (applied to a stream) rapid.

strin, strinn *n* a thin narrow stream of water etc.; the channel of a river; water in motion, smaller in extent than what is called a *stripe*.

string *n* a tide; a current.

string-of-tide *n* a rapid tideway.

strintle, strinnie *n* a very small stream.

strintle, strinnie *v* to trickle; to flow in a small stream.

stronachie *n* a stickleback.

strype *n* a small stream, a rill.

strypie *n* a very small rill.

sualter, swalter *v* to flounder in water.

sun-fish *n* the basking shark.

sun-saut *n* salt made from sea-water.

swash *n, v* the noise made by a salmon when he leaps at the fly.

swatter *v* to move quickly in any fluid, generally in an undulating way; to swim close together in the water, like young ducks.

swaw *v* (applied to the swift motion of fishes) to produce waves; to break the smooth surface of water; to cause a motion in the water.

swawin o' the water *v* the rolling of a body of water under the impression of the wind.

sweal, sweil *v* to whirl around; (used of water) to eddy

swechynge *n* a rushing sound, as that of water falling over a precipice.

sweevil *n* a swirl; an eddying movement.

swelchie *n* a seal.

swelth *n* a gulf; a whirlpool.

swift *v* to reef, as a sail.

swilkie *n* a large swirlpool in the sea.

swim *n* a state of great wetness; a flooding.

swine-fish *n* the wolf-fish.

swish *n, v* a rush of water, and its sound; a slight fall or sprinkling of water; of the wind, to blow loudly and fiercely.

swow *n, v* the dull and heavy sound produced by the regurgitations of the dashing waves of a river in a flood, or the sea in a storm.

sye *n* the sea; a coal-fish.

T

tack *v* the act of catching fishes.

taed-spue, -red *n* the seed or spawn of toads, found in stagnant water in clots or masses like bunches of grapes.

taft *n* the thwart of a boat.

tail-net *n* the herring net first shot and furthest away from the boat.

tamer *n* the sharp-nosed eel; the broad-nosed eel.

tang *n* a species of seaweed; a tangle.

tang-fish *n* the seal.

tangie *n* a sea-spirit which, according to popular belief in Orkney, sometimes assumes the appearance of a small horse, at other times that of an old man, (perhaps) the same with *sea-trow*.

tap-flude *n* high flood.

tarn *n* a mountain lake.

teak *n* an otter.

thorny-back *n* the thornback, a fish.

tibric, tibrick *n* the young of the coal-fish.

toot-net *n* a large fishing-net, anchored.

travisch *v* to sail backwards and forwards.

trink, trenck *n* a small course or passage of water; a drain.

trot *v* (used of a stream) to flow briskly, to run with noise.

tuck *n* a jetty on the side of a river.

tug-whiting *n* a species of whiting, a fish.

tymbrell *n* a small whale.

U

ullier *n* the water which runs through a dunghill.

undeip *n* a shallow place.

underbod *n* the swelling of the sea

under a floating object.

undersook *n* an undercurrent flowing against that on the surface.

unicorn fish *n* the name given by our seamen to a species of whale.

unspoken water *n* water from under a bridge over which the living pass, and the dead are carried, brought in the dawn or twilight to the house of a sick person, without the bearer's speaking either in going or returning: the modes of application are various – sometimes the invalid takes three draughts of it before any thing is spoken; sometimes it is thrown over the house, the vessel in which it was contained being thrown after it. The superstitious believe this to be one of the most powerful charms that can be employed for restoring a sick person to health.

usquebae, usqueba, usquebaugh, uisge beatha *n* water of life; whisky.

V

vaddle, vaadle *n* a shallow pool, a pool at the head of a bay that fills and empties with the flowing and ebbing of the sea.

verter-water *n* water found in the hollows of tombstones and rocks, a charm for warts.

verter-well *n* a well possessing medicinal virtues.

W

waar *n* sea-wrack.

waarcaist *n* a heap of sea-wrack.

waar-strand *n* a beach on which seaweed is cast up.

waefleed, wamflet *n* the water of a mill-burn, after passing the mill.

wall *n* a wave.

wallee, well-ee, -ey *n* a spring

in a quagmire; a spring or pool of water; the orifice of a well.

wall-girse, wall-girse-kail, well-grass, well-kerse *n* water-cress.

wally *adj* billowy; full of waves.

wample *n, v* the motion of an eel; an undulating motion.

wan *adj* (used of water) black, gloomy.

ware *n* the seaweed called *Alga marina*, sometimes *sea-ware*.

income ware *n* weeds cast in by the sea, as distinguished from those which adhere to the rocks.

warry *adj* of or belonging to *sea-ware*.

wat, wate *adj* wet.

water *n* a river, or pretty large body of running water; any body of running water, whether great or small; a wave; the ground lying on the banks of a river the inhabitants of a tract of country watered by a certain river or brook.

gae down the water *phr* to go to wreck; to be totally lost.

water-burn *n* the phosphorescence of the sea.

water-deevil *n* a water-sprite; a *kelpie*.

water-dog, -mouse, -rotten *n* the water-rat.

water-draucht *n* the outlet of water from a loch.

water-cow *n* a water-sprite inhabiting a loch.

water-custom *n* the custom of going to a well near midnight on 31st December to draw the first water of the new year, supposed to bring good luck for the year.

waterfast *adj* capable of resisting the force of rain. We now, in the same sense, use water-tight.

water-foot, -fit, -neb *n* the mouth of a river.

water-horse, -kelpie *n* the spirit of the waters.

water-mouth *n* the mouth of a river.

water-wraith *n* the spirit of the waters.

wath *n* a ford.

wattie *n* an eel.

wauchie *adj* swampy.

waw *v* to wave; to float.

way-goe *n* a place where a body of water breaks out.

wed *v* to leap out of the water, as trouts catching flies.

wefflin, wefflum *n* the back-lade, or course of water at the back of a mill-wheel.

weil *n* a small whirlpool.

weilhead *n* the vortex of a whirlpool.

wele, well *n* a whirlpool.

well-head *n* the spring from which a marsh is supplied.

well-strand *n* a stream from a spring.

wheel *n* a whirlpool or eddy.

white horse *n* the fuller ray, a fish.

white-spate *n* a flood in which the water is not muddy.

wick *n* a creek; a small bay or inlet of the sea; an open bay.

willie-pourit *n* the spawn of a frog before it assumes the shape of one; a tadpole.

wimple *v* (applied to a stream) to move in a meandrous way.

wrak, wraik, wrack, wreck, wrek *n* whatever is thrown out by the sea, as broken pieces of wood, seaweed; often appropriated to seaweed.

X, Y, Z

yair, yaire yare *n* an enclosure, stretching into a tideway, for the purpose of detaining the fish when the tide ebbs; a sort of scaffolding which juts out into a river or frith in a straight line.

yair-net *n* a long net extending into the bed of a river, inclined upwards, and fixed by poles.

yare *n* a weir for catching fish.

yeddle *adj* (applied to water) thick; muddy.

yellowfin *n* a species of trout.

yellow tang *n* the knotty fucus, a seaweed.

yoag *n* the great mussel.

Part six

Walking

A

aback *adv, adj* away, aloof; at a distance.

abad, abade, abaid *v, adj* delay; abiding; tarrying.

abad *v* to tarry.

abarrand, aberand *v* departing from the right way; wandering; going astray.

adew *adj, v* gone, departed, fled.

adreich *prep, adv, v* behind; at a distance; to follow at a considerable distance.

aftergang *v* to follow.

agait *adv, adj* astir; on the way or road.

agaitward *adv, adj* on the road, used in a literal sense; in a direction towards, of the mind.

ahin, ahind *prep, adv* behind, in respect of place.

airt *v* to urge forward, pointing out the proper course.

allars *n* garden walks.

amove, amuff *v* to move with anger; to vex; to excite.

anter *v* to adventure; to chance; to happen.

arch *adj* timorous and ready to run away for fear.

areist *v* to stop; to stay.

arm *v* to give one's arm to; to walk arm and arm.

arselins *adv* backwards.

auale *v* to descend.

B

bachlane *adj* shambling.

bachle *n* a bachelor; an old, worn or twisted shoe.

bachle *v* to shamble; to wear shoes out of shape; to walk loosely or in slippers.

baigle *v* (applied to the motions of

a child) to walk or run with short steps, as if weak; to walk slowly, as if much fatigued.

bairge *n, v* an affected, bobbing walk; to walk with a jerk, or a spring upwards; to strut; (perhaps) to wag up and down.

baise *v* to move or walk with energy.

balter *v* to dance.

bang *v* to change place with impetuosity; "to bang to the dore", to run hastily to the door.

bannet-fire *n* a punishment similar to running the gantelop, inflicted by boys on those who break the rules of the game – two files are formed by the boys, standing face to face, the intervening space being merely sufficient to allow the culprit to pass. Through the narrow passage he is obliged to walk slowly, with his face bent down to his knees, while the boys beat him on the back with their bonnets.

bauckle, bauchle *v* to shamble, to move loosely on the hinder legs; to walk as those having flat soles.

bauf *v* to make a clattering noise with the shoes in walking.

bawbee-jo *n* a lover hired to walk with a girl for a shilling or so.

beat *v* to bruise the feet in walking.

beetikin *n* a hobnailed boot.

beleif *v* to leave.

bellraive *v* to rove about; to be unsteady; to act hastily and without consideration.

bellwaver *v* (applied to the mind) to straggle; to stroll; to fluctuate; to be inconstant.

bend *v* to spring; to bound.

beuchel *v* to walk with short steps, or in a feeble, constrained or halting manner; to shamble; as in "a beuchelin' body".

bemmle *n* an ill-made man; an ungainly walker.

bensing *adj* the showing of great vigour in walking, working etc.

besy, bizzy *adj* a term used concerning beasts, which run hither and thither with violence, when stung by gadflies.

bewave *v* to cause to wander or waver; to shield; to hide; to lay wait for.

bicker *v* to move quickly.

bike *v* to hive; to gather together like bees.

bilch *v* to limp; to halt.

bilcher *n* one who halts.

bilt *n, v* a limp; to go lame; to limp; also, to walk with crutches.

biltin' *v* limping, as in "biltin' awa'".

bin *v* to move with velocity and noise.

binner *v* to run or gallop, conjoining the ideas of quickness and carelessness.

bizz about *v* to be in constant motion, to bustle; a term applied to beasts which, when beset by wasps, drive hither and thither.

birl *v* used improperly, to denote quick motion in walking; sometimes it denotes the velocity of motion in whatever way.

blad *n, v* a long and heavy step in walking; a person walking with long and heavy steps; to walk in a clumsy manner, taking long steps and treading heavily.

blup *v* to reach by running; to overtake; to be caught with a storm.

bog *v* to be bemired; to stick in marshy ground.

bogstalker *n* an idle, wandering and stupid fellow; one who seems to have little to do, and no understanding.

boytoch *v* to be bad at walking through stoutness.

brade *v* to move quickly, to take long steps in rapid succession.

braindge *v* to run rashly forward; to do anything hurriedly and carelessly.

brainyell *v* the act of rushing headlong, or doing anything hurriedly or violently, and without care.

brangill *n* a kind of dance.

brattyl, brattle *v* to advance rapidly, making a noise with the feet; to run tumultuously; to make a confused and harsh noise.

brawl *v* to run into confusion; to embroil, confound; to gallop.

breese *v* the act of coming on in a hurry.

breesil *v* to come on in a hurry, making a rustling sound.

breughle *v* to be in a state of quick motion and oppressed with heat.

buck *v* walking over the same ground repeatedly; to crowd; to walk with a stately step.

buckan *v* the act of walking or crowding.

buckie *v* to walk hurriedly.

bufflin *v* rambling, roving, unsettled; still running from place to place, or engaged in some new project or other, a term generally applied to boys.

buittle *v* to walk ungracefully, taking short steps, with a *stotting* or bouncing motion.

bulwaver *v* to go astray.

bunch *v* to hobble; to walk clumsily, used of squat or corpulent persons.

C

cache *v* to wander; to go astray.

cadie *n* one who gains a livelihood by running errands, or delivering messages.

cair, cayr *v* to return to a place where one has been before.

call ca', caa, caw *v* to submit to be driven; to move quickly.

calsay-paiker *n* a street-walker.

camshauchle *v* to walk inactively or lamely.

cannie, canny *adj* cautious; prudent; slow in motion; to move slowly; soft and easy in motion, as in "to gang canny"; safe, not dangerous.

cappilow *v* to distance another in reaping. One who gets a considerable way before his companions on a ridge is said to cappilow them.

catmaw *v* to go topsy turvy, as in "to tumble the catmaw"; to tumble.

cave *v* to push; to drive backwards and forwards; to walk awkwardly; to tread heavily, as in mud or from fatigue.

cavie *v* to rear, or prance, as a horse; to toss the head, or to walk with an airy and affective step.

caw *v* to stagger in walking, a vulgar phrase used of one who is drunken, and borrowed from the necessity of following a flock of sheep from side to side, when they are driven on a road.

chorp *v* to emit a creaking sound, as shoes with water in them.

civileer *n* an inquisitor formerly appointed by the Town Council and the kirk-session of Glasgow to apprehend persons taking a walk on the Sabbath-day.

clacher *v* to move onwards, or get along with difficulty, and slowly, in a clumsy, trailing, loose manner.

claich *v* to walk in mud or wet soil in a disgusting fashion; to expectorate greatly to clear one's throat.

clamp *v, n* to make a noise with the shoes in walking; to walk on ice with "clamps" on the shoes; a heavy footstep or tread; crampons.

clamph *v* to walk heavily, as in too large shoes.

clanter *n, v* the noise made by walking in a house with clogs.

claucher *v* to use both hands and feet in rising to stand or walk.

clever *v* to climb; to scramble.

cleek *v* to walk arm in arm.

clobberhoy *n* a dirty walker, one who in walking clogs himself with mire.

clomph, clamph *v* to walk in a dull, heavy manner; generally said of one whose shoes are too large.

cloupie *n* a walking-staff having the head bent in a semicircular form.

cloupit *adj* having the head bent in a semicircular form, applied to a walking-staff.

clute, cloot *n* the half of the hoof of any cloven-footed animal; (applied to cattle) to run off, as in "to tak the clute".

clypach *v* to work in a dirty and in slovenly fashion; to walk in a dirty and ungraceful way.

clyte *v* to fall heavily.

clyter *n* an ungraceful walk, as over wet ground.

cockersum *adj* unsteady in position; threatening to fall or tumble over.

cockstride *n* a very short distance.

comera'din *v* a term used to denote the habit of visiting, day after day, with little or no interruption.

convoy *v* the act of accompanying a person part of his way homeward, or on a journey.

corbie messenger *n* a messenger who either returns not at all, or too late, alluding to Noah's raven.

creagh *n* an expedition for the purpose of forcibly driving off cattle from the grounds of the lawful owner; a kind of foray.

craw road *phr* the direct way; as the crow flies.

crook *v* to halt in walking.

crowdle *v* to crawl as a crab.

crowl *v* to crawl.

crump *v* to emit a crashing noise; to give such a sound as ice or frozen snow does, when it yields to the foot.

D, E

dacker, daiker *v* to search; to stroll, or go about in a careless manner, not having much to do; to go about in a feeble or infirm state; to continue in any situation, or to be engaged in any business, in a state of irresolution whether to quit it or not, as in "to daiker on"; to hang on; to jog or walk slowly up the street, as in "to daiker up the gate"; to follow.

daddle, daidle *v* to be slow in motion or action; to waddle, to wriggle; to be feeble or apparently unfit for exertion; to tipple, as in "to daddle and drink"; applied to one addicted to prostitution.

dair awa' *v* (applied to sheep forsaking their usual pasture) to roam; to wander.

dander *v* the act of sauntering; to roam.

dandill *v* to go about idly.

datchle *v* to waddle; to walk in a careless manner with clothes not adapted to the shape of the wearer.

dawner *n, v* a stroll; to wander, as if a person knew not whether; to saunter.

davering *v* riding or walking in a dazed condition.

deasil, deasoil *n, v* walk or movement with the sun, from east to west.

dissle *v* to run.

dyte *v* to walk crazily.

dock *v* to walk with short steps or in a conceited fashion.

docky *v* (applied to one of small stature) to move with short steps.

doddle *v, adj* to wag about; spoken of something heavy or unwieldy moving now in one direction, then in another, with an easy motion, as a little child or an old man.

dodge *v* to jog.

dodgel *v* to walk infirmly; to hobble.

doichle *v* to walk in a dreamy, stupid state.

doiter *v* to move with an appearance of stupor and indolence; to walk feebly or totter from old age.

donnering *v* walking stupidly.

dottle *v* to move in a hobbling way.

douce-gaun *v, adj* walking with prudence and circumspection; used as to conduct; prudent; circumspect;.

dreel *v* to move quickly; to carry on work with a speedy motion.

dreetling *adj* slow, without energy.

dreich *adj* applied to one who is slow in making ready to move from a place, who makes little progress in the necessary preparations.

driddle, drizzle *v* to walk slow; to dawdle; to potter about a thing.

druttle *v* to be slow in motion; to dawdle; to waste time.

dub-skelper *n* one who makes his way with such expedition as not to regard the road he takes, whether it be clean or foul; or, as otherwise expressed who "gaes through thick and thin"; used contemptuously for a rambling fellow.

durnal *v* used to denote the motion of the cheek when a flabby person runs or walks fast.

dush *v* to move with force and speed.

dwable *v* to walk feebly or with faltering steps.

dyte, dytter *v* to walk in a stupid way or with tottering steps.

ernand *v* running.

evaig *v* to wander; to roam.

F

fa' awalt *v* to fall without the power to get up again; originally applied to a sheep, hence to a person intoxicated; hence the phrase, "to roll awald".

fadle *v* to walk clumsily: to waddle.

far, rayre, fayr *n* expedition; a journey.

farand *v* travelling.

farandman *n* a traveller or voyager.

feldifair *n* one who lodges in fields; a tramp, wanderer, an outcast.

fike *v* to be in a restless state, without change of place; to move from place to place unsteadily; to dally with a female, but not as necessarily including the idea of indelicacy of conduct.

fit *v* to dance; to dance well, as in "to hae a gueed fit on the floor"; he walks at a round pace, as in "he has a gude fit"; to walk quickly, as in "pit in a fit".

fit-dint *n* a footprint.

fit-gang *n* as much ground as one can walk on.

fit-road *n* a footpath through enclosed lands.

fit-the-gutter *n* a low, loose slipper.

fitch *v* to move any thing a little way from its former place; to move by slow succussations.

fitless *adj* apt to stumble, or to fall, from debility or carelessness.

fitsted *n* the print of the foot.

fitter *v* to injure by frequent tread-ing; to make a noise with the feet; to totter in walking, applied to a child who is learning to go out, but seems still ready to fall.

fitterin *v* the noise made by fre-quent and rapid motion of the feet.

fittie *adj* a term used by school-boys or young people to denote the state of the foot when they have stepped into mud.

flatch *v* to walk clumsily.

fleggin *n* a lazy, lying fellow, running from door to door.

flichter, flychter *v* to flutter; to run with outspread arms, as children, to those they are much attached.

flipper *v* to move the hands in walking.

floggan *v* walking fast.

flotch *v* to move in a confused or ungraceful manner, and awkwardly dressed.

foot-side *v* to keep pace with, as in "to keep foot-side".

footer-footer *v* to strut like a peacock; to walk affectedly.

forray *v* the act of foraging; a predatory excursion.

forrown, forrun *adj* exhausted with running.

forswiftit *v* strayed.

foryawd *adj* overcome with weariness.

foy *n* an entertainment given one about to leave any place of residence, or to go abroad; meta-phorically, as equivalent to wishing one a good journey.

frak *v* to move swiftly.

fudder *v* to move hurriedly; to patter with the feet; to run to and fro in an excited and aimless manner.

fuddik *n* a very short person who walks with a quick, nimble step.

futhil, futtle *v* to work or walk clumsily.

G

ga, gae *v* to go, used in a general sense; to walk; to use the limbs.

gait, gate *n, v* a way; a warlike expedition; to depart, to run away, also to begin to walk out, as in "to tak the gait"; to go one's way, as in "to gang one's gate".

gallivant *v* to gad about idly.

ganandest-gait *n* the shortest road, or the easiest to travel.

gang *v, n* to go; to walk; to die; to set out on a journey, as in "gang to the gait"; a journey; a walk for cattle.

gangable *adj* (applied to roads) passable; tolerable.

gangar *n* a walker; a pedestrian; one who travels on foot, as distinguished from one mounted on horseback.

gangarel, gangrel *n* a stroller; a child beginning to walk.

gester *v* to walk proudly; to make conceited gestures.

gilliewetfoot *n* a worthless fellow who gets into debt and runs off; a running footman.

gilravacher *n* a forward rambling fellow; a wanton fellow.

gird *v* to move with expedition and force.

girg *v* to creak; to gurgle as water-logged shoes in walking.

girse-gaw'd *adj* "girse-gaw'd taes", a phrase applied to the toes which are *galled* or *chopt* by walking barefoot among grass.

gorge *v* expressing the sound made in walking when the shoes are filled with water.

gravitch *v* to gad about in a dissipated way.

gullyvant *v* to gad about.

gutter-gaw *n* a sore caused by mud etc., in one who walks with bare feet.

H

habble *v* to hobble; to walk with difficulty.

haghle, hauchle *v* to walk slowly, clumsily and with difficulty; dragging the legs along, and hardly lifting the feet from the ground.

haig *n* the designation given to a female whose chief delight is to fly from place to place, telling tales concerning her neighbours.

haigle *v* to walk as one who is much fatigued, or with difficulty, as one with a heavy load on ones back, as in "I hae mair than I can haigle wi'" or, "my lade is sae sad, I can scarcely haigle".

haik *v* "to haik up and down", "to haik about", phrases meaning to drag from one place to another to little purpose, conveying the idea of fatigue caused to the person who is thus carried about, or produced by the thing that one carries, as in "what needs you to weary yourself, haiking about that heavy big-coat where'er ye gang?".

hame-o'er *adv* homewards.

hammle *v* to walk in an ungainly manner, so as to be constantly in danger of stumbling.

hamp *v* to halt in walking; to read with difficulty, frequently mistaking or mispronouncing words; to stutter.

hamrel *n* one who stumbles often in walking; one who walks heedlessly.

han'-for-neive *adv* "cheek by jowl"; abreast; walking as in a very friendly manner.

hanyel *v* to have a jaded appearance from extreme fatigue; to walk with the appearance of slovenliness and fatigue, as in "to gang hanyellin".

hap-stap-and-loup *v* hop, skip, and jump.

hap-stumble *v* a chance stumble.

happity-kick *v* used of an ill-assorted couple, inability to walk together in step; incompatibility.

harle *v* to move onward with difficulty; to go from place to place, as in "to harle about".

hashy *adj* a slovenly person; "a hashy day", one in which there are frequent showers, so as to render walking unpleasant from the dirtiness of the streets or roads.

hatch *v* to move by jerks.

hatter *v* to gather; to collect in

crowds; to be in a confused but moving state.

hauchle *v* to walk as those do who are carrying a heavy burden.

haummer *v* to walk carelessly.

haut *v* to limp; to halt; to hop.

haut *n* an act of limping; a hop.

haut-stap-an'-loup *v* hop, skip, and leap.

haut-stride-and-loup *v* a very short distance; literally, the same with *hap-stap-an'-loup*, the sport of children.

hauter *n* one who can hop.

heather-clu *n* the ankle; what cleaves the heath in walking.

heel *v* to run off, to take to one's heels.

heesh *v* to scare away birds.

hench awa' *v* to move onward in a halting way.

henchil, hainchil *v* to rock or roll from side to side in walking, as in "a henchillin' bodie".

Heilandman's ling *v* the act of walking quickly with a jerk.

hilch *v, n* to hobble, to halt; a halt.

hill-worn *adj* weary with hillwalking.

hingle *v* to loiter.

hippertie-skippertie *adj* to run in a frisking way, as in "to run hippertie skippertie".

hirple *v* to move crazily.

hirpledird *v* to walk lamely with a bounding motion.

hirsill, hirsle *v* to move, resting on the hams; to graze; used metaphorically as denoting a gentle or easy departure by death, as in "to hirsle aff"; when the body is in a sitting or reclining posture and the trunk is dragged along by the hands or feet rubbing all the while upon the ground.

hochle *v* to walk with a short step; to shuffle or shamble in one's gait; to walk clumsily and with difficulty.

hocherty-tocherty *v* to ride on one's shoulders, with a leg on each.

hodge *v* to move by succussation; to stagger.

hodle *v* explained as denoting a quicker motion than that expressed by the verb to toddle: "to toddle is to walk of move slowly like a child, to hodle is to walk or move more quickly".

hodler *n* one who moves in a waddling way.

hoit *v, n* to move with expedition, but stiffly and clumsily; a hobbling motion.

hoozle, huzzle *v* to breathe with a sort of wheezing noise, when walking fast.

hotch *v* to move the body by

sudden jerks; to move by short heavy leaps, as a frog does.

hotchin-hippit *adj* having hips that cause clumsy walking.

hornie *n* a game among children, in which the company runs after the rest.

hottle *n* anything which has not a firm base of itself, such as a young child, when beginning to walk, the same with *tottle.*

howdler *n* one who walks in a limping, heaving manner.

humple *v* to walk lame, especially from corns or strait shoes.

hychle *v* to walk, carrying a burden with difficulty.

hypal *v* to limp; to go lame.

I, J

jamph *v* to travel with extreme difficulty, as one trudging through mire.

jamphle, jamfle *v* to shuffle in walking, as if in consequence of wearing too wide shoes.

jank aff *v* to run off.

jant *v* to go on a pleasure trip.

jauchle *v* to walk as one that has feeble joints.

jauk *adj* shoes are said to be *jauk,* when, from being too large, they do not keep close to the foot in walking.

jaukin *v* dallying.

jaumph *v* to travel.

jaunder *v* to talk idly, or in a jocular way; to converse in a roving or desultory way; to go about idly from place to place, without having any proper object, as in "to jaunder about".

jeoparty trot *v, n* a quick motion between running and walking; (perhaps) a contemptuous designation, as equivalent to coward.

jicker *v* to go quickly about any thing; to walk along smartly.

jiffle *v* to shuffle.

jirg, jurg, jurgan *v* the act of creaking; the sound occasioned by creaking shoes; that caused by walking over a quagmire.

joater *v* to wade in mire.

jouk, jowk *v* to incline the body

forward with a quick motion.

jow *v* to move from side to side.

juffle *v* to walk hastily; to move with an irregular gait.

juffler *n* a shuffler.

juffles *n* old shoes worn with the heels down.

K, L

kibble *adj* smart at walking.

knoit, knite, noyt *v* to amble or hobble in walking.

laing *v* to move with long steps.

lamp *n, v* a long and heavy step; to take long steps.

lamper *n* one who takes long and heavy steps.

land-louper *n* one who frequently flits from one place or country to another.

land-louping *adj* rambling; migratory; shifting from one place to another.

landrien *adj* in a straight course; directly, as opposed to any delay or taking a circuitous course, and as implying the idea of expedition; running directly, as in "he came rinnin landrien".

leap out *v* to break out in an illegal or disorderly way; to run out.

leather *v* to go cheerfully; to move

briskly.

leesh *v* to move quickly forward.

leg *v* to run.

leg awa' *v* to walk clumsily.

leg-bail *v* to run off, instead of seeking bail, and waiting the course of the law, as in "to take leg-bail".

lemp *v* to stride; to walk with long strides.

lep *v* to go rapidly; to run.

lesit *adj* lost.

lewder *v* to move heavily.

link *v* to walk smartly; to trip; to walk arm in arm.

loft *v* to lift the feet high in walking; to heave or lift up.

louther *v* to be entangled in mire or snow; to walk with difficulty.

loup *v* to leap; to spring; to run; to loup about; to run hither and thither.

loup-hunting *v* "hae ye been loup-hunting?", a query addressed to one who has been very early abroad, and containing an evident allusion to the hunting of the wolf in earlier times.

loup-the-dyke *adj* giddy; unsettled; runaway.

low *v* to stop; to stand still, used with a negative, as in "he never lows frae morning till night".

lowter, lowder *v* to walk heavily.

lunt *v* to walk quickly; to walk with a great spring; a great rise and fall in the mode of walking.

lyowder *v* to amble or sway from side to side in walking.

M, N

mistlie *adj* bewildered on a road.

moolie-heels *n* chilblains.

morning-bout *n* morning walk.

naig awa' *v* to move like a horse, or nag, that has a long, quick and steady pace.

netty *n* a woman who traverses the country in search of wool.

nicht-hawk *n* a large white moth; a person who ranges about at night.

nicht-hawking *v* given to roam at night.

nibbie *n* a walking staff with a crooked head, used by shepherds, like the ancient crook.

niddle *v* to squeeze through a crowd, or any narrow place, with difficulty.

noop *v* to walk with downcast eyes and nodding head.

nubbie *n* a walking-staff with a hooked head.

O

oag *v* to creep.

o'er-by *adv* at no great distance.

ourrid *v* to traverse.

outganging *v* the act of going out of doors.

out-rake *n* expedition; an extensive walk for sheep and cattle.

oxtered *v* supported under the arm; steadied or assisted in walking by means of such support, as in "he was oxtered hame".

P, Q

pad *v* to travel on foot.

padder *v, adj* to tread; a road through the snow is "padderd", when it has been often trod.

paddist *n* a foot-pad; one who robs on foot.

paddle *v* to walk slowly or with a short step; to toddle; to tramp about in wet and mud.

paidle *v* to walk with quick short steps, like a child.

paidlin *v* wandering aimlessly.

paighled *adj* overcome with fatigue; (perhaps) wearied with carrying a load.

paiker *n* a *calsay paiker*, a street-walker.

palmer *v* to go about feebly from place to place.

pap *v* to move or enter with a quick and unexpected motion; to go from place to place with an elastic motion, as in "to gang pappin about".

pathlins *adv* by a steep path.

parrach *v* to crowd together.

patter *v* to move with quick steps, especially referring to the sound.

pawmer *n* one who goes from place to place, making a shabby appearance.

pedrall *n* a child beginning to walk.

pense *v* to walk conceitedly, with measured step.

peeling *v* travelling on a windy day, with light clothes on.

piddle *v* to walk with quick, short steps.

pinner *v* to move quickly and noisily.

pinning *v* running quickly.

pirrie *v* having a tripping mode of walking; walking with a spring; to follow a person from place to place, like a dependent.

platch *v, n* to make a heavy noise in walking; a plain-soled foot.

pleesk *v* to dash and wade through water.

pleuter *v* to wade through water or mud.

plout *v* to splash; to fall with a splash suddenly; to wade through water or mud.

pleuch-fittit *adj* having heavy, dragging feet.

pod *v* to walk with short steps.

prick *v* to run as cattle do on a hot day.

prod *v* to move with short steps, as children.

put on *v* to push forward; to increase one's speed; (applied to riding or walking) often to go at full speed.

quave *v* to go zig-zag up or down a brae.

R

rache *n* a dog that discovers and pursues his prey by scent; a poacher; a night wanderer.

raik *adj, v* the extent of a course or walk, hence *sheep-raik* and *cattle-raik*; a swift pace; the act of carrying from one place to another; the extent of the fishing-ground; the direction in which the clouds are driven by the wind.

rake *v* to range, to stray; to roam, to wander; to walk about late at night; to walk with a swift pace.

rakyng *v* (perhaps) wandering.

ram-rais, ram race *n* the race taken by two rams before each shock in fighting; a short race in order to give the body greater impetus before taking a leap; the act of running in a precipitous manner, with the head inclined downwards, as if to butt with it.

ramp *v* to trample.

raxter *n* a long walk.

reel *v* to travel, to roam; to go to and fro in a rambling and noisy way; to romp.

reel-fittit *adj* having the feet so turned inwards that when one walks he crosses his legs and makes a curve with his feet.

reenge *v* to move about rapidly, with great noise and bustle, as in "she gangs reengin throw the house like a fury".

riddin *adj* cleared off; driven away.

ride the beetle *phr* to walk with

others who ride.

rin *v* to run.

rin ahin *v* to run at one's heels, or behind; to follow closely; to fall into debt.

rin-aboot, rinabout *n* a vagabond; one who runs about through the country.

rin-the-country *n* a fugitive; one who flees the country for his misdeeds.

rink about *v* to run from place to place; to gad about.

rink *n, v* a course; a race; the act of running.

royt *v* to go about idly.

rowt *v, n* (perhaps) to range.

S

sair pechin' *v* sorely panting.

salie, saly *n* a hired mourner, who walks in procession before a funeral.

sant *v, adj* to disappear; to be lost.

schawlde *adj* shallow.

sclaff *v* to lift feet in a clumsy way, as if one's shoes were loose.

sclatch *v* to walk heavily.

sclidder *v* to slide to the right or left, when one intends going straight forward; particularly applicable to walking on ice.

sclowff *v* to walk with a heavy tread like a flat-footed person.

sclute *v* to fall flat; to walk with the toes much turned out.

scleutch *v* to slouch; to walk in a

dirty, slovenly manner.

Scotch-convoy, Scots-convoy *n, v* the accompanying of a visitor the whole way home.

Scotch cuddy *n* a pedlar; a travelling draper.

scouff *n* a male jilt; a giddy young fellow who runs from one sweetheart to another, as in "a scouff amang the lasses".

scour *n* a quick walk.

scoyloch *n* an animal which plaits its legs in walking.

scrall *v* to crawl.

scrieve *v* to move swiftly along.

scushle *n, v* an old, thin, worn out shoe; to make a noise, by walking with shoes too large, or having the heels down.

searcher *n* a civil officer formerly employed in Glasgow to apprehend idlers on the streets on Sunday during public worship.

seggit *v* walking heavily and stumbling from weariness.

shachle *v* to walk in a shambling or knock-kneed fashion.

shak a foot *v* to dance.

shauchle *v* to walk with a shuffling or a shambling gait.

shevel *v* to walk in an unsteady and oblique sort of way.

shochles *n* legs, used

contemptuously, (perhaps) originally applied to limbs that were distorted.

shoone *n* shoes.

sidle *v* to move in an oblique sort of way, like one who feels sheepish or abashed.

skellop *v* to run fast.

skelp *v* to move quickly on foot; denoting quick motion on horseback.

skelper *n* one who strikes with the open hand; a quick walker.

skemmel *v* to walk as one that has not the proper command of his legs; to climb or walk over slight obstructions, such as tables or wooden benches; to climb over rocks or walls.

skemmling *v* to romp; to throw things about in a careless or slovenly way; a foolish way of throwing the legs.

skevrel *v* to move unsteadily in a circular way.

skeyg *v* to move nimbly in walking; in quick motion, as in "at the skeyg".

skiff *v* to move lightly and smoothly along.

skilt *v* to move quickly and lightly.

skimmer *v* to flicker, as applied to light; to act or walk quickly, (perhaps) to move with the rapidity of a ray of light; to glide lightly and speedily, as one does over boggy ground when afraid of sinking, applied to the flight of a swallow near the surface of smooth water.

skirrivaig *v* to run about in an unsettled way.

skite *v* the act of slipping or sliding in walking.

sklitter *v* to walk or work in slovenly fashion.

skloy *v* to slide on ice.

sklufe *v* to trail the shoes along the ground in walking.

sklute *n, v* large clumsy feet, possibly from *klute*, a hoof; to set down the feet clumsily, or trail the shoes along the ground in walking.

skrim *v* to scud, to move quickly.

skurrieman *n* a wandering fellow.

skute *v* to walk awkwardly in consequence of having flat soles.

sladge *n, v* a sloven; one who muddies his clothes in walking; to walk through mire and dirt in a lounging, slovenly way.

slaiger *v* to waddle in the mud; to walk slowly, used contemptuously.

slaister *v* to move clumsily through a miry road.

slatch *v, n* to dabble among mire; a day when one has to drag the legs through mire.

sling *n* a long walk.

sling *v* to walk with a long step.

slonk, slonking *v* the noise feet make when sinking in a miry bog; also, when walking with shoes full of water.

slork *v* to walk through snow in a state of dissolution. It respects the sound made in consequence of the regorging of water in one's shoe.

slutch *v* to move heavily, as in a deep road.

smook *v* to go from place to place, in a clandestine manner, in order to pilfer any thing that is exposed.

snaik *v* to sneak; to walk or move furtively and secretly; to walk or work slowly or indolently.

snauchle *v* to walk in a slow and lingering mode.

snodge *v* to walk deliberately; to sneak; to slink; to creep; to tread easily; to go softly.

snoove, snuve *v* to move smoothly and constantly; to walk with an equal and a steady pace; to sneak off, as in "to snuve awa'".

snyte *v* to walk feebly.

sneir *v* (perhaps) move swiftly.

snuit *v* to move in a careless and inactive manner, with the appearance of stupor.

socy *n, v* a person who walks with a manly air; to walk loftily.

sove *v* "to sove awa' hame", to go home quickly.

sowloching *v* wallowing in a mire like a sow.

spacier *v* to walk; to march.

spank *v* to move with quickness and elasticity.

spanker *n* one who walks with a quick and elastic motion; a tall, well-made woman; a fleet horse.

spartle *v* to move with velocity and inconstancy; to leap; to spring; to splutter.

spelder *v* to toss the legs awkwardly in running.

speil, spele, speil *v* to climb.

spedlin, spodlin *n* a term applied to a child learning to walk.

spirl *v* to run about in a light lively way.

splatch *n* "a splatch o' dirt", a clod of mud thrown up in walking or otherwise.

splerg *v* to splash in walking in mud.

splorroch *n, v* the sound made by walking in wet mud.

splunting *v* running after girls under night.

spoonge *v* to go about in a sneaking or suspicious way, so as to excite suspicion, as in "there he's gauin spoongin' about".

sprackle, spraikle *v* to clamber.

spraint *v* to run, or rather spring forward.

sprattle *v* to scramble.

sprauchle *v* to climb with difficulty; to force one's way through underwood or any similar obstruction.

sprend *v* to spring forward.

sprent *v* sprung; darted forth.

sprinkil *v* to move with velocity and unsteadiness, or in an undulatory way.

spritt *v* to leap; to run off suddenly and quickly.

sprunt *v* to run among the stacks after the girls at night.

spurrie-how *v* to run as fast as a sparrow-hawk flies.

spynner *v* to gallop; run or fly swiftly.

squeengy, squeergy *v* to wander, as a dog, from place to place.

stage, stairge *v* to saunter; to walk about, rather in a stately or prancing manner.

staggrel *n* a person who staggers in walking.

staig, staik *v* to stalk with a slow, stately step; to walk where one should not be found.

staive *v* to go about with an unstable and tottering motion; to go about aimlessly.

stam *v* to strike down with the feet with violence in walking; to walk forward in a furious manner, as in "to gang stammin'".

stap *v* to step; to advance.

stap awa' *v* to die.

stappin-stane *n* a stepping stone.

startle *v* to run wildly about, as cows do in hot weather, as in "I saw the foolish auld brute, wi' her tail o' her riggin, startling as fast as ony o' them".

staup *v, n* to take long awkward steps; to walk as a person does in darkness when uncertain where he is going to place his footstep; a long awkward step; a tall awkward person, as in "haud aff me, ye mackle lang staup".

staupin' *v, adj* stalking awkwardly; awkwardly tall.

staver *v* to saunter; to walk listlessly; to totter; to stagger; to stumble; to wander.

staverall *n* a bad walking, foolish person.

stay *v* to lodge; to dwell; to reside.

stauk, stawk *v* to stalk; to hunt game; also, to walk with a high and proud step.

stech *v, adj* to puff; to be out of wind, as when one goes up hill.

steg *v* to stalk.

stend *v* to spring; to rise to elevation; to walk with long elastic strides.

step *v* to go away, depart; to pass over.

step-over *n* a footbridge; a short distance across.

stevel *v* to stagger into a place into which one ought not to go; to walk as one who, at every step, is on the point of stumbling.

stibble *v* to stumble.

stiggy *n* a stile, or passage over a wall; a stair; a flight of steps.

still as a stap *adj* quite still.

stilp *v* to step; to walk; to go on crutches; to stalk; to walk with long strides.

stite, styte *v* to move about in a stiff and unsteady way, it is said of an old man who still moves about that "he's aye stytin about".

stog *v* to walk heedlessly on with a heavy, sturdy step; to plant the feet slowly and cautiously in walking, as aged or infirm persons do.

stoit *n, v* a springing motion in walking.

stoit *v* to stagger; to totter.

stoitle o'er *v* to fall over in an easy way, in consequence of infirmity, without being much hurt.

stoor *v* to move swiftly.

STIGGY

stot *v* to rebound from the ground; to bounce in walking; quick or sudden motion; a leap or quick motion in dancing; to stumble; to stop.

stouff *v, n* to walk lazily and heavily; the act of walking with such a step; the sound of such a step.

stour *v* to move quickly from place to place, implying the idea of great activity, and often of restlessness of mind; to move swiftly, making the dust or water fly about.

stouter *v* to stumble; to trip in walking.

straddle *v* to stroll; to wander about aimlessly.

stravaig, stravaug *v* to stroll; to go about idly.

stravaiger *n* one who wanders about idly; a stroller; one who leaves his former religious connection.

stravaiging *v* the act or practice of strolling; strolling about, generally in a bad sense.

stray *n, adj* lost; not at home; strange.

stretch *v* to walk majestically, used in ridicule.

striffle *v* to move in a fiddling or shuffling sort of way; often applied to one who wishes to appear of importance.

string *v* to move off in a line.

strodd, strowd *v* to stride along; to strut; to walk fast without speaking.

strummel, strumbell *n* a person so feeble that he cannot walk without stumbling.

strunt *v* to walk sturdily.

stumple *v* to walk with a stiff and hobbling motion.

stye *v* to climb.

sugg *v* to move heavily, somewhat in a rocking manner.

swatter *v* to move quickly in any fluid, generally in an undulating way; to move quickly in an awkward manner.

swaver *v* to walk feebly, as one who is fatigued.

sweill *v* to move in a circular way.

swig *v* to wag; to move from side to side; to walk with a rocking sort of motion.

T

taiglesum *adj* what detains or retards; a road which is so deep, or so hilly, that one makes little progress, as in "a taiglesum road".

taik *n, v* a stroll; a saunter.

taiver *v* to wander.

tiawe, tew *v* to amble.

taissle, tassel, tassle, teasle *n* the fatigue and derangement of dress produced by walking against a boisterous wind.

taiver *v* to wander; to rave as mad.

tak the foot *phr* to begin to walk as a child.

tak the gate *phr* to set off on a journey.

tarsie-versie *v* a term applied to walking backwards.

thud *v* to rush with a hollow sound; to move with velocity; to beat; to strike; to drive with impetuosity.

tig *n* a game among children, in which one strikes another and runs off. He who is touched becomes pursuer in his turn, til he can *tig* or touch another, on whom his office devolves; used of cattle, to run hither and thither, irritated by flies or boys.

tine *v* to be lost; to perish in whatever way.

tipper *v* to walk on tiptoe, or in an unsteady way; to totter.

tipperty *adj, v* unstable; to walk in a flighty, ridiculous manner, as in "to gang tipperty-like"; applied to a young woman who walks very stiffly, precisely, or with a mincing gait.

todle, toddle, tottle *v* to walk with short steps, in a tottering way; to purl; to move with a gentle noise.

totch *v* to move with short quick steps.

trachle *n, v* a fatiguing exertion, especially in the way of walking; to drag one's self onwards, when fatigued or through a long road.

traik *v* to go idly from place to place; to wander so as to lose oneself, chiefly applied to the young of poultry; to follow in a lounging or dangling way.

traikit-like *adj* having the appearance of great fatigue from ranging about.

traissle *v* to tread down; to make small roads through growing corn, as in "to traissle corn", to trample it down, as in "to traissle gerse etc.".

tramp *v* to tread with force, with a heavy step; to walk as opposed to any other mode of travelling.

tramper *n* a foot-traveller, used in a contemptuous way; a vagrant.

tranont, tranoynt, tranownt, tranent, trawynt *v* to march suddenly in a clandestine manner; to march quickly, without including the idea of stratagem or secrecy.

transe *n* a passage.

trant *v* to travel.

trauchle *v* to walk as if trailing one's feet after one; A person is said to *trauchle* corn or grass, when he injures it by treading on it.

tred *v* to track; to follow the footsteps of an animal.

treissle *v* to abuse by treading.

trod *v* to trace; to follow by the footstep or track.

troddle *v* to walk with short steps, as a little child does; to purl; to glide gently.

trootle *v* to walk with short quick steps.

trow *v* to roll over, as in "to trow down a hill", to descend a hill, as children often do, by rolling or whirling.

truntle *v* to roll along.

turse *v* to walk; to take oneself off quickly.

tyce *v* to move slowly and cautiously; to walk softly.

tyning *v, adj* the act of losing; the state of being lost.

tynt *adj* lost.

U

up-by *adv, prep, adj* (applied to an object) at some little distance, to which one must approach by ascending.

upwith *adv* "to the upwith", taking a direction upwards.

ush *v* to usher or walk before a person of rank.

V

vague, vaig *n, v* a wandering fellow; a vagrant; to roam; to wander.

vaiger *n* a stroller.

venall *n* an alley; a lane.

viage *n* a voyage; a journey.

W

wa'-gang, -gain, -gaun *v, n* departing for a foreign land; departing this life; parting, leave-taking, taking farewell before such departure; also a social gathering of friends to bid farewell.

wachle, wauchle *v* to move from side to side in walking, like a young child; to walk after a fatigued manner; walking, yet almost exhausted.

waible *v* to walk unsteadily, as one who is very feeble.

waith *v* wandering, as in "a waith horse"; roving.

waff *adj, v* solitary; wandering alone; denoting the awkward situation of one who is in a strange place where he has not a single acquaintance.

waff *v* to wave; to fluctuate; to wander.

wake *v* to wander.

walit *adj* travelled.

wallop *v* to move quickly, with much agitation of the body or clothes; to gallop.

wamble *v* to move in an undulating manner.

wamfle *v* to move like a tatterdemalion, whose rags are flapping.

waukfere *adj* able to go about, as in "he's gayly fail't now, but he's still waukfere".

wauner *v* to wander.

waver *v* to wander.

way-ganging, -going *v* departure.

wear *v* to move towards a place with caution.

wegglie *adj* waggling; unstable; having a wriggling motion in walking.

wielding *v* (perhaps) running wild; (perhaps) bewildering himself.

whid *v* to move nimbly and lightly, without noise.

whiddle *v* to proceed with light, rapid, motion; to flutter as birds at pairing-time.

whig *v* to move at an easy and steady pace; to go quickly.

whilliewhallie, whiltie-whaltie *v* to dally, to loiter.

whinkin *v* walking with a saucy air.

whip aff, whip awa' *v* to fly off with velocity; to move briskly.

whitter *v* to move with lightness and velocity.

wilsum *adj* in a wandering state; implying the idea of dreariness and of ignorance of one's course.

windle *v* to walk wearily in the wind.

wisk away *v* to move off nimbly.

wingle *v* to move with difficulty under a load; to wriggle; to walk feebly.

wrabil *v* to move in a slow, undulating manner, like a worm; to wriggle.

wudscud *n, v* a mad romping boy or girl; to run away with precipitation.

wungall *n* a tumour on the sole of the foot, filled with a watery humour, occasioned by walking in tight shoes.

wynd *n* an alley; a lane.

X, Y, Z

yauchle *v* to walk with a shuffling gait.

Sources

Donaldson, D. (ed.), *Supplement to Jamieson's Scottish Dictionary*. Paisley, Alexander Gardner, 1887

Jamieson, J.J., *A Dictionary of the Scottish Language*, abridged from the Dictionary and Supplement, in four volumes quarto, by John Johnstone. Edinburgh, William Tait, 1846

Warrack, A. (ed.), *The Scots Dialect Dictionary*. London, W. & R. Chambers Ltd, 1911

Boym, S., *Nostalgia and its Discontents*. The Hedgehog Review, Vol. 9, No. 2, 2007

Macleod, I and McClure, J. D., *Scotland in Definition, a history of Scottish dictionaries*, Edinburgh, John Donald Short Run Press, 2012

Shepherd, N., 'The Weatherhouse', in *The Grampian Quartet*. Edinburgh, Canongate, 1996

Steven, H.M. and Carlisle, A., *The Native Pinewoods of Scotland*. Edinburgh, Oliver and Boyd Ltd., 1959

Acknowledgements

The first iteration of this book was a set of handmade artist's books that formed part of the practice element of a PhD supported by the Forestry Commission, the University of the Highlands and Islands, and Highlands and Islands Enterprise. A hearty thank you to all who let me accompany them in their work, and to all those who've shared their knowledge of the land with me. Thanks also to all at Saraband for their faith, vision, hard work and meticulousness, and to Kathryn Haldane, Eilidh Sutherland and Vicky Smith for their work on the book.

Thanks also to friends and family, to David for *rigwelted*, and finally to EKR – long may we flochter.